The MIT Press Essential Knowledge Series

THE FUTURE

NICK MONTFORT

The MIT Press | Cambridge, Massachusetts | London, England

This book was set in Chaparral Pro and DIN Pro by Toppan Best-set Premedia Limited. Printed and bound in the United States of America.

Library of Congress Cataloging-in-Publication Data

Names: Montfort, Nick, author.
Title: The future / Nick Montfort.
Description: Cambridge, MA : MIT Press, 2017. | Series: The MIT Press essential knowledge series | Includes bibliographical references and index.
Identifiers: LCCN 2017019916 | ISBN 9780262534819 (pbk. : alk. paper)
Subjects: LCSH: Future, The.
Classification: LCC BF327 .M66 2017 | DDC 303.49--dc23 LC record available at https://lccn.loc.gov/2017019916

10   9   8   7   6   5   4   3   2

The best way to predict the future is to make it.

Alan Kay

CONTENTS

SERIES FOREWORD

The MIT Press Essential Knowledge series offers accessible, concise, beautifully produced pocket-size books on topics of current interest. Written by leading thinkers, the books in this series deliver expert overviews of subjects that range from the cultural and the historical to the scientific and the technical.

In today's era of instant information gratification, we have ready access to opinions, rationalizations, and superficial descriptions. Much harder to come by is the foundational knowledge that informs a principled understanding of the world. Essential Knowledge books fill that need. Synthesizing specialized subject matter for nonspecialists and engaging critical topics through fundamentals, each of these compact volumes offers readers a point of access to complex ideas.

Bruce Tidor
Professor of Biological Engineering and Computer Science
Massachusetts Institute of Technology

It might be appropriate if this page, and all the others, were blank. It's often said that the future is an unwritten book. This book, however, is not itself the future, even if you have selected it as your near-future reading. I have not tried to summarize here all of the important and often contradictory ideas about the future that have been expressed so far in human culture, all throughout history. It would be hard to do so, even in the most telegraphic way, in a short book of this sort, and a commentary truly adequate to the task might not fit in any book. Instead, I offer a discussion of how the future has been productively imagined, mainly in Western culture and particularly in the United States. My focus here is on ways that the development of technologies (particularly computing and media technologies) have been bound up with ideas about the future—how future-making has been part of the development of computing and digital media, and how computers have also prompted new hopes and ideas about the future.[1]

In this book, I seek to show that it is possible to imagine the future systematically and in sufficient detail, that one can share the imagination of the future with others, and that it is possible to work to develop specific innovations that are components of such a future. By doing so, people, communities, and organizations can influence what lies ahead of all of us. This is not a view of the future as a fog-enshrouded landscape or as something seen in a crystal ball. The future as I discuss it is more like an unwritten book. We can't just think about how to view it—we need to write it. The future is not something to be predicted, but to be made.

That's a powerful idea. Of course, researchers, writers, inventors, and others do try to make new futures all the time. But the idea that the future is inevitable, something that can at best be predicted, is actually quite prevalent culturally. If we look ahead to the future only to react, we might be able to improve our chances for survival—but to what end? If we take a view of this sort, dominated by prediction, we give up on many of our own abilities and dreams, trying at best to surf toward profit on a sea of change or perhaps simply trying to avoid drowning in it.

Of course there are good reasons to develop and use predictive powers. If we can determine that an asteroid is going to collide with the Earth, perhaps we can send a drilling crew into space to destroy it. Or, to leave the absurd aside for a moment, after predicting that our climate will change due to human industry and activity, we could decide to do everything possible to stop or reverse that trend. It's appropriate to predict both those occurrences that are out of our direct control—natural catastrophes—and those that are consequences of our action. But a concept of the future that involves only prediction and reaction, rather than the development of goals and progress toward them, is incomplete. Tracking hurricanes may be prudent, but it is not all we should be doing regarding the future, and will not serve for the development of a better society.

This book was developed specifically for the MIT Press Essential Knowledge series, considered as a part of this series from the beginning. As I have written it, I've tried to always keep the focus on what I consider essential knowledge about the future. There are certain academic activities and business practices that deal quite explicitly with the future, known variously as futures studies, futurology, and scenario planning. To those who find these endeavors useful: very well. This book is not about them, however.[2] The most essential approach to the future, from my perspective, is found in future-making. Specifically, it's seen in the already-existing work of writers, artists, designers, inventors, and other innovators who developed and detailed the core components of futures they envisioned. It's also found in the continuing practices of these recent and current future-makers.

I work as a critic and theorist, and as a maker of poetry, digital art, and related sorts of work, in the field that has been called *new media* and *digital media*. My teaching and discussions with people motivated me to write this book. Over the years, as I've discussed this digital media field with a variety of people, including many students, I have found they often develop rather skewed and unhelpful views of the work of new media pioneers such as Vannevar Bush (author of the essay "As We May Think") and Ted Nelson (author of *Literary Machines* and *Computer Lib/Dream Machines*). Even those who have closely read the work of these thinkers, and who think quite favorably about these early contributors to the field, often conclude that they were good at predicting some things—for example, they predicted certain aspects of hypertext and the World Wide Web quite accurately, quite impressively—but that they unfortunately failed to predict other things.

This is a bit like saying Thomas Edison predicted the light bulb but failed to predict certain things about it. As it happens, in these cases, neither Bush nor Nelson developed complete public systems that would typically be considered working predecessors to the World Wide Web; they did not complete and illuminate the practical, everyday bulb that we use today in the most material sense. (The same cannot be said about some others I will discuss in this book, such as Douglas Engelbart and Alan Kay; they did build the future of digital media by producing working systems that people used.) Without actually completing the present-day World Wide Web, Bush and Nelson have nevertheless clearly been makers of the future, not just predictors of it. Rather than mumbling vague notions and exhortations, they provided blueprints for the development of networked information systems, helping to lead computing to where it is today. We are living in their future.

By the way, Thomas Edison wasn't the first one with a light bulb, any more than Henry Ford was the inventor of the car. Bulbs had been lit up long before Edison started working on developing one in 1878; Alessandro Volta even showed off a glowing wire, without a bulb around it, all the way back in 1800. What Edison invented, after a lot of trial and error, was a *practical* light bulb that could be manufactured, sold, and widely used. Trial and error is an important technique that leads to new developments, but having imagination, vision, and deliberate goals is important as well. Making the future can seldom be done without a plan and prototype, and if the idea is to work toward an intentional future, such a vision is particularly important. The 90 percent perspiration may be the larger share of success by far, but producing that is just exercise unless it is mixed with 10 percent inspiration.

In this book, I discuss future-making of several sorts, with my particular emphasis on those types of future-making that are involved with computing and culture. The essential knowledge I am trying to uncover in this discussion is not limited to a particular field of inquiry or to particular practices of invention and art. It is an understanding of how the future has been constructed and how we, today, can continue constructing it. As I identify types of future-making that have been done effectively, I will highlight and summarize the underlying principles and ideas that are at play. These, as best as I can identify them, are the essential points for those who aim to be future-makers—whether they are entrepreneurs, inventors, activists, artists, writers, or otherwise directed ahead.

FACING THE FUTURE

His eyes are staring, his mouth is open, his wings are
spread. This is how one pictures the angel of history.
His face is turned toward the past. Where we perceive
a chain of events, he sees one single catastrophe that
keeps piling ruin upon ruin and hurls it in front of
his feet. The angel would like to stay, awaken the
dead, and make whole what has been smashed. But
a storm is blowing from Paradise; it has got caught
in his wings with such violence that the angel can no
longer close them. The storm irresistibly propels him
into the future to which his back is turned, while the
pile of debris before him grows skyward. This storm
is what we call progress.[1]

So wrote Walter Benjamin, referring to a drawing by Paul
Klee and supplying the foundation for critical writing that

has been growing skyward in past decades. My reason for bringing Benjamin's angel into the current discussion does not have to do with history, war, rubble, or the way a series of events can appear as a single catastrophe. Rather, I find it interesting that we mortals are similar in certain ways to the angel of history. We, like the angel, can have knowledge of the past that is based on our experience, but do not have the same direct awareness of the future. We, like the angel, cannot resist entering the future—the future becomes the present at objectively the same rate for all of us, as long as we are still alive. Perhaps the angel's orientation toward the past will seem unusual, but what it is able to see rings true to our experience, and it should also seem apt that it is being drawn into the future.

The angel's orientation might seem perfectly appropriate to speakers of the Amerindian language Aymara, who live in the Andes. In this language—and, so far as modern cognitive scientists know, only in this language— the future is conceptualized as being behind the speaker, while the past is in front.[2] Speakers of all languages, as far as we know, frame time in spatial terms. A typical underlying metaphor is of journeying into the future. On a journey, one knows what is behind, all that has already been visited, but not what lies ahead. Those who communicate in Aymara are apparently unique in considering the future to be behind them, but their perspective on time and the future is not completely inscrutable. They simply use a less dynamic metaphor, considering the future as unseen, the past as being known and evident—just as what is before them is evident. In this way, they agree with everyone else about an important aspect of the future: It is unknown.

We imagine that a person traveling forward into the future, walking along, is in a very different situation than an angel being drawn backward. But even if our underlying concept is a journey—and this seems to miss an important aspect of time, that it continues to run on regardless of what we do—even in that case, the terrain is there in front of us and we can, at best, choose a route or choose our own adventure. A more powerful metaphor was offered by Joe Strummer, lead singer of The Clash: "The future is unwritten."[3] Not just unwritten in the sense of an unwritten history, in the way we might lack documentation of something that has already happened, but uncomposed and unimagined, yet to be made. This is the concept of the future I select.

We hear mixes of metaphors that involve these future concepts quite often in political discourse. In concluding his first inaugural address, President Barack Obama said: "Let us answer the call of history and carry into an uncertain future that precious light of freedom." While these were stirring words, they present the future as a dangerous darkness to be carefully explored. This does not make for the most empowering concept of the future. Earlier in this speech, Obama had said that "we reject the belief that America must choose between caring for the generation that built this country and investing in the generation that will build its future." While this expression was more conventional and prosaic, concerned with caring and investment, the future is actually described in a more empowering way here. The underlying metaphor is that we must work to construct it. We are not to poke around with the light of freedom and see what is out there in the dark, but to build what and how we choose.

I'm calling the act of imagining a particular future and consciously trying to contribute to it *future-making*. This term is meant to distinguish a potentially productive perspective on the future (let's build a better future) from a less productive one (let's predict what will happen, for instance, so we can react quickly by anticipating it). There is another important distinction to be made between working at incremental sorts of invention, necessary as this may be at times, and more radical thought and development, which may be more significant, if also more dangerous. This is between seeking a future that seems plausible and one that may be exaggerated beyond belief, or that takes some turn into what looks absurd. All of these ways of considering the future will be part of my discussion.

What's the point of an implausible idea—for instance, one in which faster-than-light travel is possible, transporter beams disassemble and reassemble people, and a

I'm calling the act of imagining a particular future and consciously trying to contribute to it *future-making*. This term is meant to distinguish a potentially productive perspective on the future (let's build a better future) from a less productive one (let's predict what will happen, for instance, so we can react quickly by anticipating it).

tiny universal translator device can interpret between any languages, even ones that aren't known to begin with? If one wants to develop a specific blueprint for concrete action, imagining a world (or universe) like this one, the world of *Star Trek*, doesn't seem to make much sense. But there are other reasons for imagining the future. Our imagination might inspire us to improve our world in way that would be hard to do by only thinking incrementally and plausibly. We might see a world in which exploration and building connections with other cultures is at least as important as military action. We might see a world in which scarcity, and even money, are greatly reduced in their significance and instead of seeking power through force, people (of all sorts) focus on discovery, development, and improving society.

I think there are many more subtle points to the utopian world of *Star Trek*. Again and again, it's shown how the universal translator or even knowledge of a language, held in common, does not resolve cultural differences—they have to be worked through consciously and respectfully. This seems like a good point to keep in mind as, powered by immense data sets and machine learning, our own translation capabilities approach those of the universal translator. In the world of Starfleet, scare resources and militarism still exist to challenge a mostly peaceful and hopeful galaxy; it's just that addressing these issues is not always done in a framework of colonialism or conquest.

The people of this universe are also as concerned with understanding their past as imagining their future.

Perhaps it's not fair to point to a well-respected science fiction franchise whose cultural influence is vast, and which goes far beyond just provoking viewers to think differently. But a long history of outrageous future visions shows that such imaginations can indeed pertain to our world, and can sometimes be more effective because of their distance from our present day and the way they exaggerate. Because of this, although I will keep a focus on computing, digital media, and related technologies, the future-making that interests me and that I will discuss will range from more plausible sketches of the years immediately before us to much more extreme imaginations.

Escape from the Kitchen of Tomorrow

As we move to consider specific historical examples of future-making, I'll describe one concept that, however prosaic, cuts across time. It is one that bears directly on the home and domestic life. If we're looking for the future within our homes, I suggest heading to the kitchen. In Gaston Bachelard's *The Poetics of Space*, the imaginative potential of the attic and cellar are discussed at length, but almost nothing is said about the kitchen, which I believe best focuses our hopes for the future. The bathroom may be similarly clean and futuristic-looking, but it is a private space, which perhaps is why "bathroom of the future" doesn't have much of a ring to it. We have many kitchens of the future to choose from, however. The Museum of Modern Art even put on an exhibit in 2010, *Counter Space: Design and the Modern Kitchen*, showing documentation of several of these. The project of advancing the kitchen into the future is one that brings together art/design approaches, technology, consumer-focused concerns, and the broader social world, so I will use this example to conclude my initial discussion of the future, to show how new types of future-building can be more limited or might break free of certain cultural concepts.

The kitchen is our maker space, where new technologies are particularly welcome, whether they are to be used for sous vide cooking or to hermetically store kimchi. We had a standing desk in our kitchen long before we had one in our home office. Smart refrigerators (the kind that order food when you're low on staples) were iconic of ubiquitous computing in the home, as it was imagined early on. The kitchen can be closed off, a separate room with a door setting it apart, but very often is open to guests, as a part of the social life of the house. The kitchen is even charged with both creative and destructive potential: As police officers responding to domestic violence calls are well aware, the kitchen is the place that offers the widest range of improvised weapons. Because the kitchen also offers dangers, even in ordinary use—from fires, being cut on blades, being pierced by broken glass, or suffering injuries from blenders and food processors—this part of the house also has plenty of room for improvement, for better safety as well as better functionality.

Kitchens have been run for the upper classes by domestic servants, have been considered the proper place for midcentury U.S. housewives, and are now getting harder to maintain as truly usable parts of the house as more people in the United States are moving to smaller living quarters in cities. The kitchen is therefore involved in social issues of class, gender, and urban life as well as serving as a technology showcase. In the mid-twentieth century, it's certainly the case that "kitchens—futuristic or not—are thick with messages about the cultural meanings of feminized domestic labor and about prevailing understandings of the relationship between women and technology."[4] The way kitchens are imagined also, of course, has to do with people's relationship to food and the industries that supply it. It's hard to just add technology to a kitchen without having some idea of how people's social lives are changing and should change in a broader context. Some would even say that this social context looms much larger than the technologies that are usually our focus—as one image of the kitchen of tomorrow suggests (figure 1).

Figure 1 Barnes & Reinecke (Chicago, established 1934). Publicity photo for Future Kitchen scale model. Silver gelatin print. Architecture and Design Study Collection. Photo: Charles McKinney, Chicago, c. 1946.

In 1944, as World War II neared an end and companies began to wonder about what would be done with the return of consumer demand, Libbey-Owens-Ford Glass developed "Tomorrow's Kitchen." This was a design based on what new properties of glass could accomplish—as with a famous video that I will discuss in chapter 8. It was one of many kitchens of the future. Among other things, this one offered to almost eliminate most cookware by having everything—even a waffle iron—integrated into the countertops. The few pots and pans that would still be needed would stow away and could be used as serving dishes.

This kitchen was documented in *Life* magazine, and its virtues were extolled there and in other news articles. For instance, the *Uniontown Morning Herald* noted that "between meal times and without the help of a magic wand the kitchen can almost instantly be transformed into a gaily-decorated play-room for the children."[5] Sounds like a great repurposing of the most weapon- and hazard-filled room in the house, particularly given that one would have to kick the kids out when it's time to cook.

In 2015 at the New Museum Triennial, the collective DIS presented a different sort of kitchen of the future, in their installation *The Island (Ken)*, a functioning kitchen island that allows a woman to relax and bathe herself in flows of water as she also washes lettuce (see figure 2).

This project is rather hilarious, but it isn't hard to see that the functions of this installation are based on stereotypical feminine activities—the comforts of a self-pampering bath, the ease of food preparation for the family. *The Island (Ken)* just takes what consumer society already thinks of women's activities in the home and brings these notions together in a convenient package. Yes, it's especially funny when the function of bathing, relegated to the bathroom, is joined with one from the more public and social kitchen. But any kitchen of the future,

Figure 2 DIS, *The Island (KEN)* (2015). In collaboration with Dornbracht. Co-designed by Mike Meiré.

when designed for the woman of the past, has a tendency to amplify old ideas about where and how women should work in the home.[6]

As Rose Eveleth wrote, "No matter how far in the future we imagine, in the kitchen, it is always the 1950s, it is always dinnertime, and it is always the wife's job to make it."[7] But rather than take this observation as a reason to abandon the kitchen as a portal into the future, I'll offer a few other ideas about how to redesign this part of the house, just to get us thinking.

The Soylent closet. Instead of having an area of the house for food preparation, simply use a closet to stockpile a uniform substance, produced by a recent food startup, that has all the nutrients necessary for life. Ingesting this relieves demands on time involved with food preparation, allows one to eat at one's workstation, and to reclaim kitchen space for other purposes, such as watching Netflix.

The farm-to-table depot. Revise transportation infrastructure to make it radically easier for food to make its way from small, organic farms in the area to one's kitchen (and from there to one's table). This could be accomplished with farmshares delivered by small drone helicopters, for instance, or by more traditional means. Within the kitchen itself, the only changes would be minor improvements for easier preparation of those foods that are locally available.

Kitchen in the raw. Ovens, ranges, and even powerful hot water heaters that are capable of heating food above 50 Celsius/120 Fahrenheit are absent, given no traditional cooking is required in this kitchen for strict raw foodists. Instead, there is space to allow seeds to sprout in natural light, and surfaces on which to chop and slice food, are enhanced.

Cooperative kitchen. A galley kitchen for a small apartment that is nevertheless designed for the use of both occupants at once. The area in which it fits could be better outfitted and offer more storage, but some of this is sacrificed to accommodate two kitchen users. Commercial kitchens, of course, are set up for the use of multiple people, so the concept is hardly new.

The microbial home. The kitchen is connected to the rest of the house in a system that recycles waste water and other outputs, producing methane gas that powers parts of the system. Like the kitchen for locavores, it incorporates low-energy systems specific to storing local food, and it also includes a beehive. The result is a home that is largely self-sufficient. A functioning version of a home with this sort of kitchen was presented by Philips Design in 2011.

Of course, my suggestions (including one that has already been realized by a design firm) are mostly based on existing social ideas and constraints on consumption of food. They are not original, and in a few years, some of these may seem extremely silly. But they are nevertheless ideas that could, by being otherwise focused, escape the most housewife-confining concept of the kitchen of the future, one that plagued this room throughout the twentieth century.

My point in speculating about the kitchen in this way is that one cannot imagine better technologies just existing by themselves—not productively. Technologies, like the people who use them, have social lives, and so one must imagine the social future as well as the improvements brought by better materials, better engineering, and new types of computation. As I detail the way we conceive of the future today, and the way we can try to undertake future-building, this connection between the social (and cultural, and political) world and the specifics of new, imagined technologies will be a common thread. It can be sensible to start thinking about the future in the kitchen; we just need to look beyond our existing social assumptions. And, of course, our thinking shouldn't stop there.

ORACLES, PROPHECY,
AND DIVINATION

Before we return to specifics, let's consider why we, humanity, came to think of the future as different from the past, and as different from the present, at all. Even as we celebrate very old concepts of the future, and those stock characters who see into it, we might manage to obscure how different our modern perspective on the future is from that of the ancients.

Ancient views of the future are still very much alive in our imagination today, represented in film and other media. Even when the film is set in the future, as with *The Matrix* (1999), visiting a traditional divinatory character—the Oracle—can be central to the plot. A prophetic vision of the future, seen at a physical location that inspires such visions, is also portrayed in the futuristic "long, long ago" world of *The Empire Strikes Back* (1980), in which Luke Skywalker enters a cave that enhances his connection to the future, not unlike the Oracle of Delphi. "Old man" and "crone" characters with special knowledge of the future remain staples of storytelling, allowing possible surprise to be converted into suspense as the development of the plot is revealed to us. It shouldn't be surprising, though, that these devices for good storytelling are not appropriate historical representations of how the future was seen in the distant past. These characters and incidents fit with our worldview today, and the ancients saw the future—and oracles, prophets, and divination—quite differently.

Early oracles and prophets, from early history and prehistory, are discussed in a very interesting way in Julian Jaynes's 1976 book, *The Origin of Consciousness in the Breakdown of the Bicameral Mind.* Jaynes posits that as recently as a few thousand years ago, people did not have consciousness as we experience it today. Instead, they simply acted, fully engaged with the world, in ways that did not involve the sorts of introspection that are usual now. Rather than thinking about new situations and events in the way we are accustomed to, and making decisions as we do today, they experienced auditory hallucinations from one side of their minds that advised the other side on courses of action—as if they heard the voice of a god. It was the breakdown of this previously divided mind, Jaynes argues, and the formation of the type of mind we have today, that gave rise to consciousness. There are some strong adherents to this theory today; others find the underlying concepts to be provocative and potentially useful if some of the evidence and specifics to be flawed; still others find the ideas to be of little use—opinions on this theory, we could say, are more than bicameral. However, the idea of bicamerality that Jaynes introduced is still quite present in popular culture; the influence of this theory is seen very strongly in the recent TV series *Westworld* (2016–), for instance.

One fascinating aspect of this theory of bicameralism is that, if accepted in some form, it can explain historical practices of divination, which according to Jaynes were undertaken to try to recover the god's disappearing voice. This voice is said to have become silent during this period of breakdown, when our current sort of consciousness arose. Even if cognition was improved in many ways by the change, the loss of this voice was distressing, according to Jaynes, and people sought a return to the old mode of consciousness and the way in which the advice-giving mental voice would speak. In making the case that oracles and prophets result from this cognitive change, Jaynes provides a detailed and cross-cultural look at how such voices spoke in early history and how the future was spoken about or seen by the ancients.

Bicameral voices weren't exclusively talking about the future. A prophet is often thought of as someone who foretells what is to come, but this is only one of the roles of prophecy and divination.[1] Still, the ancient prophet would have been one of the most future-oriented members of society. Techniques for divination, although they could be used to locate water or to decide who has to do an unpleasant task, were also some of the practices most involved with the future as we now think of it, even at a time when the contemporary concept of the future, and certainly of future-making, had not taken hold.

Of the four types of divination—including omens, augury, and spontaneous divination from the surroundings —a particularly interesting way to learn of divine will and perhaps see into the future is by casting lots. Jaynes explains that the meaning of this activity was quite different centuries ago. "We are so used to the huge variety of games of chance, of throwing dice, roulette wheels, etc., all of them vestiges of the ancient practice of divination by lots, that we find it difficult to really appreciate the significance of this practice historically," Jaynes writes, explaining that what we understand as "chance" is a recent invention, unknown to those who undertook these techniques: "Because there was no chance, the result *had* to be caused by the gods whose intentions were being divined."[2]

Determinism does have its adherents today, yet the concept that things happen by chance is quite prevalent in many cultures and a commonplace of everyday discussion. We might flip a coin to decide where to go eat or which movie to see—not because we expect the gods to intervene, but just because we care more about getting on with it and less about a specific outcome, and we're willing to leave the specific choice to chance. Or, we might unskillfully throw darts at the newspaper's stock listings and invest in whatever we hit. (Inspired by the book *A Random Walk Down Wall Street*, *The Wall Street Journal* did this for more than a decade, from 1988 until 2002, and their investments did rather well, although their returns didn't exceed those of stocks picked by professional investors.) We also might try to intentionally randomize our actions if we're playing rock paper scissors or are involved in some activity similar to playing this game. In playing rock paper scissors against a capable opponent, the best one can do is to make truly random moves—the Nash equilibrium of the game is for each of the two players to independently select a move at random each turn, winning 50 percent of the time in expectation. Any deviation (shifting to slightly favor rock, for instance) leaves the player open to being exploited by the opponent. In that case, for instance, the opponent could play paper all the time and win at least slightly more than 50 percent of the time.

If the concept of chance did not exist in the time of casting lots to make decisions and predict the future, however, the practice would certainly have to be understood very differently, without any sense of arbitrariness. Every predictive token would be placed deterministically; it would just be placed for a reason that is far beyond us.

Stéphane Mallarmé wrote that a throw of the dice will never abolish chance, but Jaynes believed that it did just this for the ancients, in the sense that this practice, and the culture, was without the concept of chance. This helps to explain something related in the New Testament: what it means that the selection of Matthias as an apostle was done by casting lots. Historically, it wasn't that the apostles were gambling (in the sense we think of gambling now) or leaving things to chance, in the sense that we think of chance. Rather, they were allowing for "the gods"—or in this monotheistic case, one god—to make the determination for them. Casting lots was the way to hand over the decision to divine agency.

This sort of attitude toward the future is, of course, not future-making; it isn't even the weaker predictive and reactive attitude in which different possible scenarios are considered. The future is as good as set, and people go through the motions of casting lots to allow the gods to turn them about, to be directed. Perhaps the best way to understand why people undertook this practice, consulted oracles, and listened to prophets is not to assume that they wanted to think more effectively and incisively about the future. Rather, they did this *instead of* thinking about the future. In this way, this type of decision making might be a bit like having a "torn choice" (where one alternative is about as good as the other), flipping a coin to make a decision expediently, and getting on with it rather than

Perhaps the best way to understand why people undertook this practice, consulted oracles, and listened to prophets is not to assume that they wanted to think more effectively and incisively about the future. Rather, they did this *instead of* thinking about the future.

thinking through one's future more fully. But the process wasn't exactly like that. Instead of taking the attitude that it doesn't matter either way, the ancients using processes of divination were likely thinking that what action was undertaken *did* in fact matter, and that because of this, they didn't want to decide what to do.

Why would this attitude, which seems fatalistic today, have been the case in the past? Economist and historian Robert Heilbroner holds that people of early times held a static view of their society, imaging that the future was an extension of the present, just as the past was. He argues that the idea of improving society, of a future that could be different—and indeed, of progress—was not developed until the middle of the eighteenth century. While a social organization that made change unlikely was part of the reason, there were also aspects of the prevalent worldview that related to this perspective on the future.

Many centuries ago, Heilbroner explains, as history was being developed and before there was an idea of what prehistoric humans were like, societies generally imagined themselves to be of divine origin and to have always lived in a condition similar to their current state. People were most concerned not with invention, trade, discovery, or learning new things but with the natural forces that beset them, which could threaten their lives or provide for a good harvest. Nature, and these forces, might manifest differently at different times, of course. But it was thought that nature would stay more or less the same over the years. There was no reason the future would be different.

Later, when human nature rather than the natural world became central to people's concerns, the belief in the static nature of societies persisted, with unchanging human nature taking the place of unchanging nature. Heilbroner cites Machiavelli, who wrote early in the sixteenth century: "Whoever wishes to foresee the future must consult the past; for human events ever resemble those of preceding times. This arises from the fact that they are produced by men who ever have been, and ever will be, animated by the same passions, and thus they necessarily have the same result."[3] This idea, of course, exhorts those seeking to foresee the future to look at history—but for very different reasons than we would imagine now. Reading history would not show the seeds of the current situation and help one think about how it might grow into the future. It would simply be an opportunity to look at some documentation of essentially the same stasis as that in which we currently reside, to understand people of the past who are the same as people today.

Despite our modern concept of the prophet as one who can look ahead, the ancients were not deeply concerned with even knowing the future, and certainly not with making it. As Heilbroner writes, "Resignation sums up the Distant Past's vision of the future."[4] Even though "prophecy" is used again and again in movie titles, even though we name our commercial computing systems "Oracle" and "Delphi," there is little evidence that ancient prophets and oracles were visionary leaders who helped to make the future of their societies. Whether we accept the idea of bicameral breakdown or not, such figures seem to be part of static, ancient societies, ritually handling concerns for the future without developing more profound ideas of foretelling, and certainly without developing ideas of future-making.

So, it seems that this was our early, resigned, deterministic stance. Before we can even take a predictive view of the future, and certainly before we can engage in future-making, we have to see how our concept of the future, as we know it today, actually came about.

Progress and the Current Future

To understand cultural concepts of the future, it's worthwhile to begin by contrasting a belief in stasis—that over years and generations, human society remains essentially the same—with a belief in progress. These aren't the only cultural worldviews. For instance, the early Greek poet Hesiod, departing from the view of resigned stasis, described the people of his time as being at the end of a period of decline, as being of the race of iron, the final, most base race of man. There is also a cyclical view, which in the long term is a static one but would involve improvements and downfalls. Still, the difference between a belief in a generally static social condition and a belief that things have improved, and will continue to improve, is an essential difference in views of the future. This shift is deeply involved in developing the idea of a future that can be co-constructed by members of society. My discussion of the idea of progress is not because I believe things will necessarily get better on their own, but because having *any* view that goes beyond stasis is necessary for getting to the idea of future-making.

In classical times, and even in times before, it was not really feasible to believe that one's world was in absolute stasis. The seasons caused observable changes throughout the year almost everywhere, and a winter could be better or worse, a harvest more or less abundant. But many believed that the world was generally static, only perturbed by occasional natural disasters or conflicts. There was no cultural idea that society was radically improving—or undergoing a decline—or even that progress was possible.

Perhaps inspired by the nature of the seasons and natural disasters, both Plato and Aristotle described society as cyclical. In Plato's *Laws* and in Aristotle's *Politics*, human society is described as moving from the family unit through different forms into that of the city-state, which is the political realization that allows for human excellence. Of course, this is not an idea that allows for further progress, since it names the current form of government as the best. Furthermore, the city-state cannot endure, in the view of Plato and Aristotle, so society has not progressed to a stable form, but just happens to be at this point as it makes a circuit.

This seems like an odd view, given that Plato designed a society in his *Republic*, providing the prototype for utopian writing and the imagination of better societies. But Plato didn't see that any society, even his carefully crafted one, was immune to collapse or would be able to continually improve.

The first major ancient philosopher to reject the cyclical view of society and advocate for a linear one was Augustine of Hippo. A cyclical view would have been hard to reconcile with Christianity as we understand it today. Christ's coming to earth and being resurrected, according to Augustine, were singular events. Some other Christian thinkers at the time held that they were part of an endlessly recurring cycle, but that belief ended up being condemned as heretical. Augustine's view eventually prevailed. Although these events—unique events according to Christians—resulted in redemption and improvement of some sort, there was not a particular idea of earthly progress that went along with Augustine's idea of spiritual betterment. The idea that our social conditions were improving came about during the Enlightenment, in the eighteenth century.

The concepts of the Enlightenment were developed in that century in the wake of incredible scientific achievements, beginning with Nicolaus Copernicus in astronomy. His discoveries, along with those of Galileo Galilei and Johannes Kepler, of course suggested a new relationship to the universe, one in which the Earth was not central, nor was humankind. But the work of these scientists and of Isaac Newton also showed that the efforts of many people could be brought together to produce powerful new models of the world and insights into how the world works. It became clear that the scientific method was a powerful means of learning about the world. Since this method had been recently developed and many new discoveries had been made, it made less sense to think of the world of the Enlightenment as being essentially the same as the world had been several centuries before.

Various Enlightenment authors began to develop more specific ideas of progress. Among them were the economist Adam Smith. While he did not see a completely clear path to progress, he did describe how economies, if guided by the "invisible hand" of the free-market system, would be able to improve themselves. In the nineteenth century, there were two important thinkers who saw history as a process of working through opposition toward betterment. Georg Hegel, with his idea of ideological development through the conflict of states, was one. Another was Karl Marx, who described the rise of capitalism and predicted the emergence of communism through historical conflict.

Much more can be said about the idea of progress from the Enlightenment up through today. Certainly, Smith and Marx did not agree about how social and historical progress was to happen or even about what it meant to improve society. Still, even a brief review of these Enlightenment thinkers is enough to show that the idea of stasis, that a society could be expected to remain the same over time, had been supplanted by their time, and by Hegel's.

Looking beyond the nineteenth century, some major currents of thought oppose the idea that society has truly made progress. Against the improvements (many of them, even if they were not universal) in daily life, health care, and availability of goods, we should consider that the twentieth century saw genocide and war on unprecedented scale. Today, in the twenty-first century, the human population of the Earth is the largest ever, and all of us inhabiting the planet face a series of massive environmental catastrophes that rational people understand we ourselves have precipitated. Those who think deeply about the future can no longer assume the optimistic position of Enlightenment thinkers; at least, this is hardly the automatic conclusion.

While our challenges today may include very grim ones, the shift in outlook does not affect the basic question of how we form an idea of the future. Is our society static, as if we are offshoots of the gods placed in an unchanging world? Or it is possible for things to change—for the better, hopefully, but really in any way at all? Let's allow that we may discard the philosophical optimism of the past—that scientific discoveries will automatically lead to improvement, that the free-market economy will improve itself, and that conflicts of ideas and classes will lead to revolutionary, better societies. Nevertheless, we can believe that the future will not be only more of the same, and that it will not be only that given to us by divine powers. Once we see that the future can be different, as those Enlightenment thinkers did, we can begin to think about shaping and making the future. Yes, even if we don't buy every element of the centuries-old idea of progress, the concept can help us see that change, and improvement, can be possible.[5] That is a starting point, at least, from which the more powerful idea of future-making can develop.

LITERARY UTOPIAS

Our topic now is utopian writing, which describes fictional, often ideal societies that are relevant to us today and are relevant to the future. Two seemingly unusual but venerable aspects of future-making can be noticed in the way literary utopias have been written. First, by fictionalizing a society and distancing it from news, lawmaking, and other nonfictional frameworks, it is possible to leave aside certain details and make a more powerful argument about the positive ways in which people can live together. Second, this writing allows us to see how even extreme and perhaps absurd imagination can factor into our thinking about society. There is room in a utopia for the plausible, sensible alternative to today's practices, but also for the outrageous, which can provoke our critical faculties and open our minds to unusual ideas.

One way to chart a future is to describe a society that doesn't exist, perhaps as a beacon toward which our present society might steer. An early example, already mentioned, is provided by Plato, who developed an ideal society of philosopher-kings (a community that entirely excluded poets) in his *Republic*, almost four centuries before the Christian Era. But the genre of writing we are discussing takes its name from a short book in Latin by Thomas More, *Utopia*, which was published in 1516.[1] The book isn't, strictly speaking, about the future—it describes a fictional society of that time. But it clearly suggests some ways that Western, and particularly English, society could be different in times to come. The book describes the highly systematic functioning of island residents, people who behave in many ways like monks following the Rule of Saint Benedict: They live communally, doing manual labor. More's Utopia has been described as "a communist community, enhanced by Christian values."[2]

There are a few differences from either the modern-day communist concept or monastic life, of course. Unlike a monastery, the land of Utopia is a heterosocial place, and people get married and raise children. Each person who is about to marry is presented with his or her potential partner, naked, and allowed an inspection—sensible, More explains, because one considers even a horse very thoroughly for any sign of ill health before purchasing it. It seems difficult to understand this procedure as a serious proposal, but, at the same time, it might point out that marriage is impractical between two people who know very little about each other in other ways. Why would we demand to take the saddle off the horse and inspect it closely while not giving the same concern to our betrothed?

One lesson in future-making that can be seen here is that utopian ideas don't have to be entirely serious to have some bite to them, and to be effective in provoking people to change their thinking and move toward a better future. The pre-marriage inspection can be read in several ways— as making fun of people's obsession with physical attractiveness, for instance, or as making fun of marriage as an institution that establishes ownership, like the ownership of a horse, of one person by another. (This is a plausible reading, I think, even though in More's egalitarian Utopia, both bride and groom are presented, separately, for chaperoned inspections by the other.) The inspection also points out that our concepts of human pudicity and of the modest deportment of horses are quite different, but this is probably not the first thing most readers would want to reconsider when thinking about how to reorder their society.

Utopia is almost certainly not a full-on parody of More's society. It presents an alternate society in which there are few laws, people live communally and sustain themselves by cultivating and making what they need, and people pursue learning throughout their lives. Most of the ideas are presented, as with Plato's *Republic*, as ways society could be reordered and improved. So, it's interesting to see a few cases in which the customs of the Utopians strain credulity. One effect that this can have is stimulating multidimensional thinking about current society and the way that it's organized. Another effect is that it can remind us to be critical and thoughtful. Even if we like the direction an author is taking and the type of society that is being proposed, we shouldn't accept every new idea presented as if it were a new doctrine.

American Nowheres

If we start our search for utopias from the United States, one vision, and one particular book, looms particularly large. This is Edward Bellamy's 1888 novel, *Looking Backward: 2000–1887*. Set in Boston in the year 2000, it follows the experiences of a man who, like an even more dormant Rip Van Winkle, entered a trance in 1887 and was brought out of his suspended animation in good health more than 100 years later. What he found, as the book's preface explains, was "a social order at once so simple and logical that it seems but the triumph of common sense." He tours the city, learning about the improved working conditions and the abundance of food and goods available to everyone.

Boston, and the United States, have been transformed into a bountiful socialist utopia.

Soon after the novel was published in 1888, its publisher was acquired, the book was reissued, and it became tremendously popular. A million copies were sold in two years, with only *Uncle Tom's Cabin* and *Ben-Hur* outselling the book, and in those cases over a longer span of time. Dozens of clubs were started to discuss the socialist ideas of the book. These groups, organized by "Bellamyites," were called "nationalist clubs" because of negative associations with the term "socialism," but they were closely related to the concept of socialism and did not have any particular relationship to what we now think of as nationalism. These clubs were only around for a few years, but they, and Bellamy's book, were an important influence on the Theosophical movement, which went on to establish a dozen utopian communities in the United States. The impact on American writing was strong, too, with more than 150 books being written in response to *Looking Backward*—including exuberant sequels and several books opposed to the ideas of the original novel.

Looking Backward's new society is based on ideas that precede the book; this society is also presented well in the context of the novel. The narrator, Julian West, is from the same time as his early readers, and it's of course necessary for people from the year 2000 to explain to him how this strange new society works. The difference between the improved social order and that of 1887 is illustrated throughout *Looking Backward*, but perhaps never as memorably as when the narrator finds that a sudden downpour has begun and he—and, it seems, everyone else—is without an umbrella: "The mystery was explained when we found ourselves on the street, for a continuous waterproof covering had been let down so as to enclose the sidewalk and turn it into a well-lighted and perfectly dry corridor, which was filled with a stream of ladies and gentlemen dressed for dinner." As one of the natives explains, "the difference between the age of individualism and that of concert was well characterized by the fact that, in the nineteenth century, when it rained, the people of Boston put up three hundred thousand umbrellas over as many heads, and in the twentieth century they put up one umbrella over all the heads."

Bellamy's novel presents a society of abundance in which each person is allotted a specific amount of what is produced, a bounty that is clearly greater than anyone would need but is still regulated. To mete out the many goods, Bellamy introduced what he called the "credit card," the first use of the term, although it didn't actually allow purchases on credit. Industries have been nationalized in the book, and this credit card system allows for the equal distribution of goods. Rather than paying anyone more, those who have to do particularly unpleasant work simply get to work fewer hours. Women have a more equal role in society and are part of the workforce, although "the heavier sorts of work are everywhere reserved for men, the lighter occupations for women."

Another intriguing model society, which responded to this particular aspect of Bellamy's, was presented by American author Charlotte Perkins Gilman in her novel *Herland*, originally published in 1915. In this book, three adventurous men locate an isolated community that is entirely female. (The women of Herland, it is explained, are able to reproduce without men.) The girls and women are highly accomplished at all necessary work, from tasks that are traditionally considered feminine in U.S. culture, such as child-rearing, to building houses. They prosper, eschewing rote learning, governing their society deliberately, and wearing clothing that has numerous pockets.[3]

While *Herland* does offer some suggestions as to the social order, and promotes certain types of feminist thought about society, it seems unlikely that Gilman was literally suggesting that the best society would be a secluded, nonindustrial one with only women. More likely, her plausible portrayal of women working in all roles in society was meant to show that—even in a society that has both men and women—it does not make sense to restrict women to only a few social roles. Aside from the implausibility of asexual reproduction, critics take issue with some other aspects of *Herland*, including its attitude toward native people, who are repeatedly disdained as "savages."

Despite such flaws, the novel remains a powerful work of imagination, particularly given that it was published before women even had the right to vote throughout the United States.

Utopian Future-Making

More's Utopia, Bellamy's year-2000 Boston, and Gilman's all-female society are all presented as ideal, or close to ideal, as was the republic that Plato described. Those who study utopian thought and writing distinguish, however, between a utopia or "no place" and a eutopia or "good place." A utopia is an invented society, existing beyond history as an alternative to present societies, but it doesn't have to be perfect. It doesn't even have to be better, so a fictional society that is presented as negative and deeply flawed, a dystopia, can also be seen as a type of utopia. There are also notable novels that are set "no place" and present societies that have some positive and some negative aspects; these include Jonathan Swift's *Gulliver's Travels* and Samuel Butler's *Erewhon*.

One way that utopias can function is by portraying a plausible alternative to the current social configuration. More's book prodded readers to think about how communal living without private property might be possible. Bellamy's made it seem plausible that a well-planned society could produce more than enough for everyone to live well and could happily distribute that wealth equally rather than leaving some in poverty. And, even if readers of Gilman's book didn't think that an all-female society was actually the best idea, they could probably believe many aspects of the portrayal of women working in every possible role in a community. If we can imagine such possibilities within the framework of fiction, this can make it easier to think of them in our own reality.

Even implausible aspects of utopian fiction can be useful, for several reasons.[4] They can point out, as with any satire, how outrageous our current society is. They can also encourage us to think critically as we imagine a better society. Also, they might help to expand the limits of what we consider possible. Because utopian fiction takes us away from the specifics of our current place and situation and transports us to no place, it allows us to come to new insights that can then be applied to the world we live in. Perhaps an all-female society existing for thousands of years isn't plausible, but if it were, wouldn't the women in it be capable of doing anything that was needed? If so, isn't it reasonable to allow women to occupy any role in our mixed-gender society? Utopian thinking is of course often associated with silliness and impossible, impractical ideas, but when it's done effectively, shifting our thinking from our current place to no place can help us get out of a rut.

For future-making, then, there are two useful lessons from utopian fiction:

• Abstracting away from the particularities of present circumstances, while still considering human nature, can help one develop a long-term idea of the future.

• It can be okay to mix the plausible and the implausible in thinking about the future, if there's a reason (satire, encouraging critical thought, expanding our thinking) to go beyond what is believable.

A future-maker might do something clever by coining a term or inventing something specific. This can be useful, but this is seldom as powerful as developing an overall, coherent vision that can be worked toward, engaged with deeply, or opposed. Although it's interesting to note that Bellamy is (at least approximately) the inventor of the credit card, his real influence is seen in dozens of organizations founded to think through and promote his work, and the dozens of books written to continue the conversation he started.

WORDS-IN-FREEDOM,
ART FOR THE FUTURE

Italian Futurism holds a few lessons for future-making. The founders and proponents of it, who spoke of embracing technology, actually did embrace new media technologies to get their message out. They also transgressed traditional boundaries between the arts, quite effectively. As we will see, Futurism in Italy was not without its problems. But these particular methods of future-making were not, in my view, inherently bound to the negative directions that Futurism took.

While writers of fiction have worked for centuries at developing utopias, some artists (who also write) have focused on the future in quite different ways. The art and literary movement most explicitly obsessed with the future was defined, in its original, Italian formulation, in 1908 by Filippo Tommaso Marinetti. His "The Founding and Manifesto of Futurism" was published, initially, as a two-page flyer in January 1909. In early February this manifesto was published as an article in a newspaper in Bologna. One imagines it must have been a slow news day when the newspaper ran a pronouncement by a poet, but apparently this fervent call to action was compelling to readers. The manifesto appeared again, in late February, in French translation, at the top of the front page of the Paris daily newspaper *Le Figaro*. At the beginning of the earlier document, Marinetti had added a highly unusual and figured description of a car crash, which served as an origin story for the movement.

It was a pretty radical document in its historical context—and it still is when read today. While Futurism resulted in a good deal of impressive art and literary work, and while Futurists wrote many more manifestos, the best-known contribution of the movement is likely this first manifesto. Marjorie Perloff, noting that Marinetti received more than a thousand letters after the publication of this first manifesto in *Le Figaro*, writes that "Not only are Marinetti's manifestos more interesting than his poems, novels, or even than such experimental collage-texts as *Zang Tumb Tuuum;* his *arte di far manifesti* became a way of questioning the status of traditional genres and media, of denying the separation between, say, lyric poem and short story or even between poem and picture."[1]

To give an overall sense of this document while staying specific, I'll comment on the last three items in Marinetti's list of intentions:

> 9. We will glorify war—the world's only hygiene—militarism, patriotism, the destructive gesture of freedom-bringers, beautiful ideas worth dying for, and scorn for woman.

This sounds a bit grim, and the avant-gardes that emerged after World War I began certainly had a bit of a different opinion of war, based on direct experience of it. Still, the celebration of war, purity, and violence must have sounded pretty good to some people at the time who saw themselves as living in a stagnant culture. The scorn for women might have seemed brash and appealing to some men, too, particularly if they associated women with the complacent, domestic, and maternal. Note, however, that not all of those letters that Marinetti received in response to this manifesto were supportive.

> 10. We will destroy the museums, libraries, academies of every kind, will fight moralism, feminism, every opportunistic or utilitarian cowardice.

Again, it appealed to some people that something, even war and the destruction of museums, might clear away cultural stasis and allow for a renewal of art. And, did Marinetti mention that the Futurists don't like women? Valentine de Saint-Point published an enthusiastic embrace of Futurism with a response to this aspect of the manifesto in 1912. This was her "Manifesto of Futurist Woman," in which she said virility was necessary but declared: "The majority of women are neither superior nor inferior to the majority of men. They are all equal. They all merit the same scorn."[2]

> 11. We will sing of great crowds excited by work, by pleasure, and by riot; we will sing of the multicolored, polyphonic tides of revolution in the modern capitals; ...

It's worth emphasizing that this was written almost a decade before the Russian Revolution in 1917. No revolution of this sort had ever happened in the industrialized world. Marinetti and his group were not "singing" to describe recent events or to commemorate older ones. They were envisioning a future, and at the least, they were one set of voices offering permission to the revolutionaries who were to come.

We will sing of the vibrant nightly fervor of arsenals and shipyards blazing with violent electric moons; greedy railway stations that devour smoke-plumed serpents; factories hung on clouds by the crooked lines of their smoke; bridges that stride the rivers like giant gymnasts, flashing in the sun with a glitter of knives; adventurous steamers that sniff the horizon; deep-chested locomotives whose wheels paw the tracks like the hooves of enormous steel horses bridled by tubing; and the sleek flight of planes whose propellers chatter in the wind like banners and seem to cheer like an enthusiastic crowd.

The technologies described, some well established by this time, but also airplanes and the automobile that is the main character in the beginning of this manifesto, are described as beautiful, often fast, and almost always dangerous and "violent." This last quality just made these technologies more exciting, whether it was the knife-like glitter of the bridges or a steering wheel imagined (in the first part of the manifesto) as a guillotine. Threatening to cut off—what?

This was the cry for the future that went up from technology-obsessed young men at the beginning of the twentieth century. They were young, too: "The oldest of us is thirty: so we have at least a decade for finishing our work. When we are forty, other younger and stronger men will probably throw us in the wastebasket like useless manuscripts—we want it to happen!" Destroy the museums and libraries, embrace the violent machine of the modern world. "Art, in fact, can be nothing but violence, cruelty, and injustice."

If that sounds akin to fascism, it was—Futurism and fascism in Italy were consistent in their principles, including their rejection of democracy. They became closely linked after 1918, with Futurist art produced to serve Mussolini's fascist regime. Daniele Conversi wrote that the Futurists "saluted Mussolini's ascent to power in the name of an imperial dream as Head of a New Italy ... Futurist strategies and techniques became keys to the advent of fascism as a media-driven phenomenon. Mussolini spoke openly of his debts to Futurism: 'I formally declare that without Futurism there would never have been a fascist revolution.'"[3]

Beyond that, it's not really fair to just say that there was misogyny involved in the origins of Futurism—there was a good bit of racism and colonialism, too. These are not as evident in the first manifesto, but Marinetti's 1909 novel *Mafarka the Futurist*, set in North Africa and depicting slaughter and rape, provides plenty.

To understand what the Futurists were up to— focusing only on the Futurists in Italy, although there were also rather different Russian and Ukranian Futurist movements—it's worthwhile to ask whether the future was, for this group, just a rhetorical flourish or some vague, general direction. Or was it, instead, a deep part of their thinking and art? Were they actually undertaking future-making through their creative practices? My argument is that they were, and that the future was more than a rallying cry for these writers and artists.

The Futurists are also a good example of a complicated and deeply problematic group that focused on the future. The Italian Futurists of course aren't unknown, but they don't get quite the same attention in scholarship, in exhibitions, and in the popular consciousness as do the big movements that followed, including Dada and Surrealism. Other twentieth-century avant-gardes have more palatable politics, being leftist and associated with socialism or anarchism—tendencies present in Futurism at its beginning—and typically reacting against war rather than celebrating it. Futurism, with its misogyny, racism, colonialism, embrace of violence (even after the horrors of World War I), and of course its fascist finish clearly demonstrates that thinking about the future doesn't make one morally, culturally, socially, politically, or aesthetically right. (The Futurists actually did pretty well when it came to aesthetics, though, as most agree these days.) Were there positive aspects to their concept of the future, and can they be extricated from the rest of their exclusionary, past-negating project?

Technology and Literary Art

One interesting aspect of Futurism could also be seen in Dada, a movement that started a few years after Futurism did, during World War I, and that was influenced by this earlier movement. This was an embrace of the popular. Such an embrace meant opposing the distinction between high and low culture and between fine art and mass media. The Dadaist assault on high culture, for instance, could be seen in Hugo Ball's attiring himself in a cardboard "magic bishop" costume for a ceremonial sound-poetry reading, in Marcel Duchamp's exhibition of a urinal as art, and in Duchamp's exhibition of a reproduction of the Mona Lisa with a mustache added.

While the Futurists had not aimed at the same sort of parody or employed the same sort of humor, they did embrace modern, popular communications media. Their outreach to the people was not done out of fellow-feeling or democratic ideals, but to recruit the masses to their patriotic, and later fascist, project. While the purposes of the Futurists are not wholesome, many artists, writers, and movements learned from how the Futurists transgressed the boundaries of fine art and supposedly proper, limited methods of publishing.

The publication of their first manifesto in newspapers—and its being printed as a pamphlet and distributed before that—shows this acceptance of popular media. Marinetti and others also produced other leaflets to support their cause, climbed the bell tower in Piazza San Marco in Venice, and dropped them from there. The Futurists produced poems on posters, mounted exhibitions, hosted performance evenings, and published their own newspaper-like journals. While the first anthology of Futurist poetry was rather conservative in many ways, the movement walked the walk when it came to embracing industrialized technologies to publish and distribute their work.

Literary Futurism became less conservative after another important manifesto, Marinetti's "Destruction of Syntax–Wireless Imagination–Words-in-Freedom" was published in 1913. Influenced by the way telegraph messages are written, Marinetti called for a focus on the core of language—nouns and verbs, with verbs in the infinitive—and the use of mathematical symbols. By arranging language of this sort unconventionally, and using a wider range of the typographical capabilities of the printing press, Marinetti and others produced work that had aspects of both poetry and visual art. Technology was not just an influence on the channel of distribution, but on the way words were chosen and put together. The result challenged traditional categories of artistic and literary production and reception. Unsurprisingly, that result often also celebrated war and violence, as in Marinetti's famous "Bombardment of Adrianople" from around 1914.

Marinetti and others also developed sound poems, meant to be performed or read unconventionally. One that effectively portrays a technology, and a process of writing, is Giacomo Balla's 1915 "Noise-Making Onomatopoeia Typewriter," which instructs "twelve people to each … repeat for one minute constantly the following noise-making onomatopoeia." (Balla is best known for making very significant contributions to Futurist visual art.) Investigating the mechanization of writing by simulating the din it creates, this less violent poem nevertheless deals with central Futurist concerns.

Futurist visual art was certainly significant, too. Painters in the movement used cubist techniques in new ways, and Umberto Boccioni produced remarkable Futurist sculptures. However, it is literary Futurism that most strongly shows a connection between a concept of the future and artistic practice.

While there is a good deal to repudiate about the Futurists, and while there is also plenty to admire more generally about their positive influence in art and literature, some specific lessons this Italian group offers for future-making are as follows:

• The Futurists communicated about the future using media channels and formats that were consistent with their concept of it. Their embrace of fast-paced technology extended to their use of newspapers, fliers, leaflets, and posters as media for their artworks.

• Even in their first manifesto the Futurists included artists of many types in the movement. They worked across the arts—including the literary arts and performance arts—and in the process violated the culturally approved boundaries that prevented certain sorts of innovation. In this regard Futurism was like many other twentieth-century avant-gardes, including not only Dada and Surrealism but also Fluxus. The Futurists, as with those in other movements, worked across boundaries not just to be provocative, but because they saw there were important new connections to be made. In so doing, they accomplished collaborative, interdisciplinary work of the sort that has been important for positive forms of future-making.

Where Did Futurism Go Wrong?

As my discussion of the first manifesto is meant to show, Futurism wasn't really right to begin with, although the movement did develop some good particular ways of making art and effective ideas related to future-making. Both aesthetically and in terms of politics, the Futurists wanted to make such a break with the past that their relationship to history was framed in terms of eradication and cleansing. Dada, while strongly anti-art and antiwar, took an approach of playful engagement with the dominant culture. The Dadaists continually insulted, repudiated, and denounced bourgeois art—yet, even with their fierce opposition to the status quo, they were seeking in certain ways to converse with the present culture rather than bomb it out of existence. Provocations and interventions generally turned out to be longer-lasting in memory and more effective, over the past century, than the Futurist cry to destroy museums.

While the typography of words-in-freedom was radically new, other Futurist art built on certain earlier developments, such as cubist painting. Futurist practices were not completely divorced from the history of art, despite the call to erase that history along with museums and libraries.

The Futurists saw potential in technology, but their glorification of it can be seen as accepting a type of "strong" or "hard" technological determinism. They seemed to believe that the logics of technology would, by themselves, lead on to a new phase of history and transform humanity for the better. I distinguish this view from one that admits that technology has influence, but acknowledges it as one of several aspects of culture and history, and acknowledges that technologies were developed in the first place for particular purposes. This is not to say that every

Provocations and interventions generally turned out to be longer-lasting in memory and more effective, over the past century, than the Futurist cry to destroy museums.

Futurist was as eager as Marinetti to be led on by technology. Günter Berghaus explains that members of the group also identified a "machine angst": "The Futurist machine god had a Janus face, one side divine and positive, the other obscure and frightening, and too painful to be admitted to the conscious mind."[4] Still, consciously and under the leadership of Marinetti, the main impulse of Futurism was to embrace and celebrate contemporary technologies. They sought to be driven by the automobile more than to drive it.

Given these flaws, can anything be learned from the Futurist example? The use of modern-day communication technologies (of the same sort embraced by Futurism), the development of new artistic practices based on such embraced technologies, and making connections between stereotypically separate artistic practices—it is hard to see how these elements of future-making are exclusively tied to the negative aspects of the Futurist ideology and outlook. The enthusiasm with which the Futurists embraced technology may have related to their attitude of hard technological determinism, but, even in this case, it is possible to imagine a deep engagement with technology that is critical.

While I've tended to dwell on the problematic aspects of Futurism—these are among the main reasons I have written about the movement—it's worth noting that nationalism and the celebration of war were not inherent to every Futurist vision. In one text, for instance, Balla envisioned the future as made pure through light, geometry, and new ideals, describing the future as "an immense extremely prismatiridescentriluminous diamond, extremely clean, elegant, lived in by the most beautiful, dazzling humanity, very spirited, ordered, happy, extremely healthy, spiritualized by new IDEALS ... and with an indestructible superfaith; see you soon in a few centuries."[5] Balla's typewriter-imitating sound poem is also a good example of Futurist work that accepts modern technology, and explores it, without promoting nationalism or violence. Finally, among Balla's paintings are remarkable landscapes, done in a Futurist style but without glorifying even technology at all, and certainly not war.

Perhaps one fairly recent car crash between Futurism's technologically extreme attitude and the playfulness of Dada can be seen in an online forum—a Usenet newsgroup, specifically—that was active in the 1990s. The people who posted to this group, alt.pave.the.earth, advocated that the entire earth be paved so that people could easily hurtle about in their extremely fast-moving automobiles. While those posting stayed in character, the nature of the hyperbolic parody was evident to almost everyone—this was not a Futurist celebration, but a discourse making fun of those who were driven by technology. Some, I suspect, may have read a few of the posts and started to question the need to further pave their parts of the earth—rather than trying to establish more compact, walkable cities or provide good mass transit. While the Futurists used their extreme visions to whip up giddy interest, similar visions can also be used to provoke thinking, including critical thinking. Even the hyperbole of the Futurists shouldn't be dismissed as a means of future-making. It could be used to help put on the brakes, when appropriate, rather than to accelerate.

WORLD'S FAIRS
AND EXHIBITING THE FUTURE

World's Fairs provide some fascinating historical examples of how the future has been envisioned and how future visions have been shared with the public. The main lesson I see in them, in contrast with utopian writing and other types of future imagination, is that the perspective on the future that is offered—not just what in particular is imagined—is particularly important.

A remarkable aspect of the last century is that, amid world wars and standoffs between the superpowers, a powerful, elaborate means of sharing visions of the future was developed in an international context. These future visions might suffer from their often doggedly corporate direction and from their basis in excitement about new technologies, but they have offered surprisingly rich models of the future with which one could argue or agree. They presented ideas of the future more fully than disconnected slogans could have, and they showed a way to engage the future that a range of thinkers have since employed. And, interestingly enough, one of the standout exhibits from the world's fairs was quite concerned with the automobile—as were the Futurists, as were the denizens of alt.pave.the.earth—in a less violent and extreme way, certainly, but, still, with this automotive technology as central to the vision of the future.

My specific focus here will be the famous Futurama exhibit sponsored by General Motors at the 1939–1940 World's Fair, one that returned in a different form to the 1964 New York World's Fair. It was an extremely popular exhibit, and while it focused on a near-term vision of the future, it epitomized the future-oriented world's fair exhibits of the twentieth century. I'll describe the historical context, and legacy, of Futurama and describe what lessons this exhibit, and those similar to it, have to offer for future-building.

Before Futurama, before even the officially designated world's fairs, there were national exhibitions, initially taking place in France and then extending throughout Europe, meant to encourage and showcase technological improvements.[1] The tenth such exhibit in France, the French Industrial Exposition of 1844, was particularly influential and prompted similar expositions in six other cities, from nearby Bordeaux to Saint Petersburg. It was most significant, however, for influencing the first truly international event of this sort, one open to exhibitors from anywhere in the world. This was London's Great Exhibition of the Works of Industry of All Nations, held in 1851.[2] The Great Exhibition is now considered the first world's fair. It took place in one of the most famous temporary buildings of all time—perhaps outdone only by the Eiffel Tower, which was built for another world's fair—resonantly named the Crystal Palace, an impressive technological showcase formed from a glass roof and facade, as if it were an early version of an Apple Store (see figure 3).

Figure 3   The Great Exhibition in the Crystal Palace, Hyde Park, London: The transept looking north. Steel engraving by W. Lacey after J. E. Mayall, 1851.

This was accomplished with a skeleton of cast iron and a new method of casting plate glass. Just shy of a million square feet in size, the Crystal Palace enclosed not only what approximately fourteen thousand exhibitors were displaying on eight miles of tables but also, with a ceiling surpassing a hundred feet, numerous fountains and trees. The building was both a pristine technological showcase and a sort of greenhouse that could be placed without damage to the site in Hyde Park. (It was designed by Joseph Paxton, a horticulturalist.) A visitor might imagine that the industrial development represented by this sheltering building could coexist with nature—or that it could frame and control nature. The four main categories of exhibits—raw materials, machinery, manufacturers, and fine arts—allowed for cultural exchange that went beyond the advancement of technology. Six million people attended the Great Exhibition, including Charles Babbage, Charles Darwin, and Charles Dickens, just to mention a few who had the same first name.

The Great Exhibition was a great financial success and had significant intellectual and political effects, promoting internationalism, trade of raw materials between countries, and further industrial development. The famous building, although it no longer stands, endured for a while, too. It was dismantled after the exhibition and erected on a different site, in South London, where it stood for more than eighty years until a fire destroyed it.

The Great Exhibition was an auspicious start to decades of events that would further international contact and exchange and allow industrial enterprise to communicate with the public. These fairs showcased amazing advances. In 1876, at the first world's fair to be held in the United States—in Philadelphia—Alexander Graham Bell's telephone was shown to the public for the first time. At another U.S. world's fair, the World's Columbian Exposition held in Chicago in 1893, George Ferris tried to outdo the Eiffel Tower (built for the 1889 World's Fair) with a structure that moved, the Ferris Wheel. Back in Paris in 1900, Rudolf Diesel showed his prototype engine to the public for the first time. In 1901, in Buffalo, a working X-ray machine was first demonstrated to the public at the world's fair. And, back in Paris once again in 1914, just before the outbreak of World War I, Spanish engineer Leonardo Torres y Quevedo showed what was a partial but no doubt extremely impressive chess computer—a system that, while not capable of general-purpose computation or of playing a chess game from start to finish, could play an endgame perfectly. Inventions and technological progress were very important to these events, certainly, but it wasn't until 1939 that a world's fair explicitly focused on the future.

1939: The Future's Fair

At the end of April 1939, in Flushing Meadows, Queens, just a short drive or train trip from the nerve center of Manhattan, a world's fair opened with a new sort of theme, based not only on the future but also, quite specifically, on future-making. The slogans for the fair were "Dawn of a New Day" and "Building the World of Tomorrow." There were pavilions representing sixty countries, including particularly impressive contributions by Russia, France, Poland, and Britain (housing the Magna Carta, which had left the United Kingdom for the first time). The Jewish Palestine Pavilion introduced the concept of a Jewish state, which would later become Israel.

Even if one could somehow miss out on the international perspective, there was much of interest for those from the host country and for other, international, visitors at this world's fair. The Westinghouse "Moto-Man," Elektro, provided robotic performances for audiences. Immense modernist structures were erected. In a convergence of different sorts of future-making, the First World Science Fiction Convention was held at the fair. This world's fair had been planned, in part, to help lift New York City out of the Great Depression, although it did not post a profit and there were plenty of complaints, beginning before the fair opened, about how costly all the preparations were. The fair, which ran two seasons, did garner a great deal of mindshare, attracting forty-four million people.

The cultural legacy of this internationalist event is even more remarkable given that it ran for just over four months before a new, much more grim day dawned on the world—in the form of World War II. On September 3, 1939, Great Britain and France declared war on Germany, the only major country that did not participate in the 1939–1940 World's Fair. Two weeks later, Germany invaded Poland.

Nevertheless, in that moment, those few months, before the war, advances in technology and in imagination continued, and in ways that are still instructive to us today. Representative of this was the General Motors exhibit Futurama, the most popular at the fair. It depicted a vision of only twenty years into the future, one largely enabled by new types of highways. This was certainly a utopia that included lots of product placement—the automobile played an essential role in it—but it was also a rich and systematic imagination of the future that was sensitive to human needs and social life. The designer behind the exhibit, and the follow-up book, *Magic Motorways*, was Norman Bel Geddes, an industrial designer who had also extensively designed for theater and the movies.

Futurama was seen by five million people. Ironically, given that the exhibit was largely about eliminating congestion, the line for Futurama sometimes extended more

Ironically, given that the exhibit was largely about eliminating congestion, the line for Futurama sometimes extended more than a mile.

than a mile. Bel Geddes attributed the popularity of the exhibit to the topic: nearly all of the visitors drove cars or rode in them and were concerned about the future of transportation. Futurama, an immense diorama, depicted highways running efficiently along modeled sections of terrain that were based on aerial surveys and broadly representative of the United States. This exhibit offered a detailed, practical proposal for much better automotive travel. It introduced the concept of limited-access, divided expressways to the public, celebrating the work of civil engineers as well as car companies.

The automobile was, of course, the central technology in Futurama, but cars didn't clog population centers; the centers of towns and cities were shown as open to pedestrians, with vehicle access restricted. The diorama also depicted new agricultural methods, new forms of power generation, and even some new flying vehicles. An impressive new technology—one that was actually prototyped by 1960, although not deployed—was a fully automated highway system that would allow drivers to relax as it brought moving vehicles closely together to efficiently travel long distances.

Practical concerns, related to their own everyday use of cars, may have motivated visitors to wait in line, but it was no doubt the spectacle of the diorama and the novelty of the presentation that made the long wait worthwhile. Seated in upholstered chairs that were moved along rapidly by a conveyor system, visitors viewed the diorama below through glass. There were sound and light effects along the course, which ran for a third of a mile.

The perspective of Futurama was like that of a third-person, top-down "God game" such as *SimCity*, quite different from the first-person perspective presented in Edward Bellamy's *Looking Backward*. Both were compelling visions of the future, quite influential in United States history, but they couldn't have been more different in how they were presented—not because one was an exhibit and the other was a novel, and not even because one was twenty years in the future and the other more than a century, but because one offered a nearly omniscient view while the other featured a protagonist being introduced, personally and at street level, to a new type of society. In terms of the utopias imagined, there were some connections. Just as Bellamy envisioned a single "umbrella," an array of awnings, that would cover everyone, Bel Geddes envisioned a single roadway strip of light that would replace individual headlights and keep glare out of motorists' eyes. Of course, there were differences between these visions too, but the differences in how they were presented were the most striking.

Between the very different, and yet successful, perspectives of Bellamy's novel and Bel Geddes's exhibit, it can't be that one of these is always the best approach for presenting one's future future-making. Adnan Morshed made the argument that the critical transportation technology in Futurama is not the car (with its enhanced highways), but the airplane.[3] While airplanes were used to survey terrain and help construct a diorama representative of different parts of the United States, even more important was the spectator's unusual perspective for viewing this exhibit, from above, moving steadily—as if seated on board a plane. From this vantage point, it seemed as if the country and its transportation systems could be fully grasped and that a designer could set things right by developing needed infrastructure and bringing flows of people into harmony.

Bellamy's ground-level and personal vision was of a different sort, and suitable for someone whose focus was on daily human life and on improving social welfare. He showed the interpersonal and emotional plausibility of his system, something that was not as important when considering a national system of smoothly running expressways. Bellamy argued that what we value about our way of life and our day-to-day experiences could be sustained, and could prosper, in the new system he envisioned. He used a kind and knowledgeable guide to offer the background necessary for understanding what his narrator saw and experienced, in his fictional, utopian world of a future Boston.

Bel Geddes, on the other hand, sought to show that his transportation advances could work in any region of the country. His focus was on one specific problem with social dimensions, that of congestion, which limited people's mobility due to slowing, inefficient traffic. Showing traffic flowing smoothly and rapidly everywhere was more important, in this context, than giving a personal perspective on the society of twenty years hence. The bird's eye view may have overlooked some street-level benefits that could also have been developed in Futurama's plan, but it was very suitable for looking to the main issue treated in this utopia. As Bel Geddes mentioned, almost everyone visiting Futurama would already drive or at least ride in cars, so people arrived with a personal stake in the problem. What they need to be shown is how the system can change.

One of the things to learn from General Motors, Bel Geddes, and the spectacular diorama of 1939:

• The future that is constructed matters, but so does the perspective from which it is portrayed. However a future is presented, it should show enough of how a system works and make enough of a personal connection to resonate.

Further Fairs, Beyond the New Futurama

The 1939–1940 World's Fair in New York was not the last of the world's fairs, but it did conclude one era of these

The future that is constructed matters, but so does the perspective from which it is portrayed. However a future is presented, it should show enough of how a system works and make enough of a personal connection to resonate.

international events. There was another world's fair that also was open in 1939 and 1940 in the United States—this one, the Golden Gate International Exposition in San Francisco, celebrating the completing of that city's bridges. Oriented toward the Pacific, it was also shadowed by the war. Treasure Island, the artificial island on which the Golden Gate International Exposition took place, was converted into a naval base soon after the fair ended.

World's fairs in the twentieth century continued to focus explicitly on the future. In 1958, the Brussels World's Fair featured the Philips Pavilion, designed by Le Corbusier, which offered a multimedia presentation composed by Edgard Varèse, one of the first fully electronic compositions. Seattle's Century 21 Exposition in 1962 was the occasion for construction of the Space Needle and a monorail; this fair celebrated scientific achievement and the space race. The World of Tomorrow exhibit, for example, was seen by about a hundred visitors at a time, who rose through it in a hydraulic device called the Bubbleator.

The 1964 New York World's Fair soon followed, on the same site as the 1939–1940 fair and sporting the 120-foot-tall Unisphere. This was a globe formed from a stainless-steel grid, encircled by space-age traces of orbits and surrounded by fountains. While many governments within the United States and many U.S. companies participated, the fair was not approved as official by the Bureau of International Expositions and did not feature as much international involvement. Pepsi presented a pavilion that introduced Disney's famous "It's a Small World" ride.

This time around, General Motors once again had an immense exhibit hall. The company presented an updated version of Futurama in which people were portrayed moving about on the moon, visiting the ocean floor, conquering terrain in new ways, and traveling through changed cities using novel transport—such as moving sidewalks. People exited from the new Futurama to the Avenue of Progress, where they learned how engineering was done at GM. This fair prominently featured computer technologies and the space age, but also had a war looming over it. Before the first season closed, Congress passed the Gulf of Tonkin Resolution, approving the United States' military involvement in Vietnam.

Another success story for cultural exchange and impact was Expo 67 in Montreal, with the theme "Man and His World." The fair celebrated the 100th anniversary of Canada's founding. More than sixty countries participated, and more than fifty million people attended. The fair far exceeded expectations for attendance, and also did much better than expected financially. However, that meant a loss of only a bit more than $210 million Canadian. World's fairs draw tourists to the host city, but they are usually money-losing events even when things go better than planned. Seattle's Century 21 Exposition was a rare exception, and was actually profitable.

The difficulty of funding world's fairs is one of the reasons that large, general world's fairs, typical for the late nineteenth and twentieth centuries, haven't been held nearly as often in recent decades. Public interest and the ability to attract tourists, and companies' ability to showcase new developments outside of such events without the same expense, are cited as other reasons for the decline. Fairs are still put on, but now tend to be based on specific themes, such as energy. The next "universal" exposition is planned for Dubai in 2020.

Futurama made its last official appearance, in revised form, at the 1964 New York World's Fair, but General Motors has continued to sponsor attractions dealing with transportation. The company sponsored one of the original exhibits at Disney's EPCOT Center, a park conceived of as "a permanent world's fair." EPCOT opened in 1982, and World of Motion, the GM exhibit, presented the history of transportation. It also had a post-ride area of displays, similar to the Avenue of Progress, which educated people about how GM designs and engineers cars today.

GM's exhibit at EPCOT was open through 1996; since the end of the 1990s, General Motors has had the Test Track at EPCOT, allowing visitors to design cars and experience a simulation of riding in them. The orientation of General Motors exhibits turned to history and then narrowed on the present day, while the perspective taken became more individual and first-person. Instead of surveying a systematic design for a national highway system or a city's transportation network, the visitor is given a personal view of one simulated, customized car and what it is like to drive it. While this may serve the interests of the sponsor, from the purpose of future-making, this shift in perspective does not seem auspicious.

THE PRE-INVENTION OF THE WEB

Probably even more familiar to us today than the Interstate
Highway Network, which was formed, post-Futurama,
beginning in the 1950s, is our World Wide Web, a global
information system that is now accessible instantly not
only at workstations and notebook computers, but also
on phones. This system carries a tremendous number of
commercial interactions along with an unprecedented
store of information, and it also has a recognized inventor.
Tim Berners-Lee proposed this system early in 1989 and
implemented enough of the system to load the first Web
page later that year. He did have support from others on
the project, including Robert Cailliau, but Berners-Lee's
work and vision were at the core of the Web, and he is its
first author.

The World Wide Web (and the future-making work
that preceded it) holds several important lessons for

future-makers. As is particularly clear in considering Douglas Engelbart's work and his predecessor hypertext system, an effective vision of the future is one that is engaged with society and builds on personal experience. Engelbart's vision, like Ted Nelson's concept of hypertext, involved higher-level concepts connected to specific, concrete ideas and examples. An effective vision is one that can scale up to widespread use and to new types of use, for instance, by groups of collaborators. Such a vision can draw on utopian modes of thinking and description, and can be exhibited directly as well as described and discussed in writing. And as for the Web itself, related to and in contrast to Vannevar Bush's early system and some of Theodor Nelson's rich concepts of hypertext, this system took root because it was simple enough to be adopted, and because it was open and available to everyone.

Berners-Lee dedicated the Web to everyone in world, asking for no royalties, filing for no patents, and ensuring that Web technologies would be unencumbered and free for anyone to use. Instead of becoming a monopolistic system limited to those in wealthy countries with financial resources, the Web—even if aspects of it present problems at times—has, as advertised, become remarkably worldwide and open to all sorts of businesses, universities, organizations, and individuals.

While much more could be said in praise of Berners-Lee, I am going to look back at how the foundation was laid for the success of the Web, a success that began in the 1990s. One way to excavate what underlies the Web involves looking at the Internet, and its predecessor, the Arpanet. Many people don't even distinguish between the Web and the Internet nowadays, but in a technical sense the Web is distinct from and carried upon the foundational network that is the Internet. Email makes its way through the Internet without using Web protocols. Yes, many people now use Web-based email, reading and sending messages with a Web browser, but the Web is not crucial, even in those cases, to the transmission of email. Teleconferencing, for instance on Skype, is often done via the Internet but not using the Web, and peer-to-peer file-sharing services are Internet-based without being Web-based. Pulling apart the Internet and the Web will also show that the success of the Internet, which provided the essential ways to convey data from computer to computer, has been essential to the Web's success. However, my exploration of what precedes the Web is not a look at the history of the Internet, but a look along another dimension of the Web's foundation.

What I will discuss here is how the core concepts of the Web were developed—what led to the idea, and the reality, of a hypertextual network of information, based on but not limited to text, connected by links, developed by a wide variety of people, and distributed across privately administered servers. Three of the most important future-builders contributing to the World Wide Web were Bush, Engelbart, and Nelson. Bush laid out a vision for a global, interconnected information system in 1945. Engelbart worked through the 1960s to create the oN-Line System (NLS), a working computer system with hypertext capabilities and many more remarkable features. Nelson developed a hypertext system starting in 1967; he also articulately advocated for an information landscape of interacting "literary machines," laying out detailed plans.

While the Web may have been invented in 1989, it didn't come to fruition in a year, and, generally, the future isn't built in a year. The concepts of a linked, interconnected information network that directly underlie the Web were developed over a period of about half a century. They were sketched out and in many cases realized, initially, on a smaller scale. Actually, much of Berners-Lee's process of invention could be described as stripping away complexity from powerful and elaborate systems, from more intricate projects that couldn't have been as widely and freely adopted in as little time. Building the future is not just adding new ideas, but can also be a process of determining which ones are essential.

The main writings I discuss here, about the important predecessors to the Web, can be found in complete or excerpted form in *The New Media Reader*, a book I coedited with Noah Wardrip-Fruin. That book also reprints the

While the Web may have been invented in 1989, it didn't come to fruition in a year, and, generally, the future isn't built in a year.

first official publication about the World Wide Web, and it includes an important publication about the Dynabook project, the project discussed in chapter 7.

Vannevar Bush's Memex

Among other distinctions, Vannevar Bush developed an important analog computer, served as the first dean of engineering at MIT, headed the Carnegie Foundation, and went on to work as President Franklin Delano Roosevelt's science advisor during World War II. He worked, perhaps harder than anyone else, to establish what would be called, years later, the military-industrial complex. This configuration has also been called the military-industrial-academic complex, as the research and teaching that happens in universities is an important component of it.

While Bush's early analog computer, the differential analyzer, was an important invention, his most influential invention was described in a popular article but never completely constructed and tested. It also did not explicitly involve a computer, even of the analog sort. This was the Memex, which Bush envisioned beginning in the 1930s but described most fully in *The Atlantic Monthly* in July 1945, in an article entitled "As We May Think." (An abridged version of the article was reprinted later that year, with striking illustrations, in *Life*.) Bush admired Allied scientists for coming together during the war for a common cause; he also saw a need for a peacetime project to provide a way to continue this collaboration that would advance humanity. The Memex, a system to advance knowledge, extend the library, and further collaboration among scholars, was his proposal for a type of Manhattan project that, instead of being weaponized, would be oriented toward the peaceful advance of knowledge.

Bush's Memex system included user-interface advances for researchers—the "scientist of the future"—but also an architecture, a sketch of a protocol, and server-side mechanisms for information storage and retrieval. One critical technology that would enable the system, Bush explained, was photography. Wearing a camera at all times, researchers would be able to casually photograph any object of interest, "without even an audible click," a capability finally provided about seventy years later by Google Glass and Snapchat Spectacles. Bush also saw advances in dry photography (later called xerography) and microphotography as being essential to the Memex; of course, these technologies did become very important to information transmission and storage.

Bush looked for other ways to facilitate the intake of information, also proposing a speech recognition system—accomplished by a combination of the Voder speech-synthesis system and stenographic recording—to

Wearing a camera at all times, researchers would be able to casually photograph any object of interest, "without even an audible click," a capability finally provided about seventy years later by Google Glass and Snapchat Spectacles.

allow hands-free commentary, which could be provided by a researcher while this person took photographs with the envisioned wearable camera. Among other things, Bush suggested that we might learn to write numerals in a more machine-readable way to facilitate data entry; the trace of this idea can be seen in the human- and machine-readable OCR-A font from the late 1960s, still in use on checks, and the shorter-lived Graffiti handwriting recognition system in Palm personal digital assistants.

All these are part of the Memex vision, and the overall system, but the interface that has become most emblematic of the system is the desk, depicted in *Life* in marvelously mechanical form, with seemingly functional file drawers underneath its complex mechanisms. The desk provided a way to consult any material that had been library processed; it would be stored in *super*microphotographic form in the desk itself and could be consulted by code number. Furthermore, hand-written notes could be photographed and added to the information store. Without describing computation, or the computer's ability for symbol manipulation, as a key component of the system, Bush nevertheless sketched out how a scaled-up form of analog indexing and retrieval could be employed to provide something very much like a Web browser—and a system for adding to the Web.

Bush proposed not only the combination and extension of existing technologies, but also how these could enable a fundamental change in the storage of information. In libraries, a book can be shelved in only one place. Cataloging systems help to group books on similar topics together by co-locating them, but because a book covering two different topics in depth can only be in one place, its ability to associate with others is quite limited. A library can also organize its books according to when they were acquired, which is less ambiguous but eliminates the conceptual benefit of co-location. Bush realized that documents in the Memex do not have to be restricted to a single place as experienced by the user. They could be organized by association—specifically, by trails of association created by researchers. A scholar could link together insights from different documents—more like developing an annotated bibliography than creating a single Web link—and this could serve to organize them for future researchers, who could contribute new associative trails themselves.

It's certainly the case that specific technology developments (wearable cameras, speech recognition) were given an important expression in this popular article by President Roosevelt's science advisor. It's also important to recognize how much the Memex vision contributed to the World Wide Web—and how there are still aspects of it (such as associative trails) which are not well implemented. At an even higher level, though, Bush's paper was influential for suggesting that the wartime technological sprint could find a more uplifting expression after the war, furthering the peacetime work of scientists as well as other types of researchers.

Bush's bold vision, compelling as it was, did not erase social divisions of the time. Any imagination of the future is situated in a social context, and while it may address certain problems within that context, it is too much to hope that disparities and injustices can all be recognized at once, much less that a solution can be proposed. Writing of the data entry that would be required to set up the Memex, Bush declares: "Such machines will have enormous appetites. One of them will take instructions and data from a whole roomful of girls armed with simple key board punches." Not only do the roles of women and men remain clear in this future vision; these girls, ready to do office work, are metaphorically "armed."

The scientist who is described creating an associative trail is researching weaponry—he "is interested in the origin and properties of the bow and arrow." Such glints in Bush's writing may be appropriate to the geopolitical era known as the Cold War that began in the wake of World War II. More than two decades after the Cold War was over, in 2014, DARPA announced a project called simply "Memex" that would search the "dark net"—online information not indexed in standard search engines—to uncover evidence of crimes online. It's safe to say that such penetrating government searchers were not essential to Bush's vision for the Memex, as he hoped that scientific advances "may yet allow [humanity] truly to encompass the great record and to grow in the wisdom of race experience."

"As We May Think" didn't escape every limitation of its time. You could say it was trapped, along certain dimensions, in the kitchen of the future. The Memex idea, as it has been to some extent realized via our World Wide Web, is powerful enough today to allow us to trace the history of many different lines of thought and topics, including, for instance, women's role in computing, not just the history of the bow and arrow. The fundamental idea of the Memex was to enable widespread information access and intake, and to organize information by multiple associations, as the human mind does. In practice, it has proven hard to limit the uses of such an associative system, even if one were to imagine that it would be used only by men or only by scientists.

Bush's *Atlantic Monthly* article certainly wasn't transmuted directly into today's Web. There were several steps along the way; the first major one was taken in the 1960s in Palo Alto.

Douglas Engelbart's NLS

When Douglas Engelbart died in 2013, the headlines of his obituaries often proclaimed him "inventor of the computer mouse," for instance in the *New York Times*, the *Seattle*

Times, *CNN*, and the *Guardian*. Computer use since the mid-1980s has almost always involved mousing—using a pointing device alongside a keyboard. There are other, alternative interfaces such as trackpads and touchscreens that are now widely used, but the mouse is hardly in danger of extinction. It became particularly popular after it was introduced as an essential, emblematic component of the Macintosh in 1984, and, while the rolling ball has given way to optical sensors, this input device remains in use in all sorts of office environments. So it might seem a positive and appropriate acknowledgment to recognize Douglas Engelbart as the inventor of the mouse. It is suitable in some ways, yet Engelbart's invention of the mouse represents only a tiny slice of his formidable contributions to computing.

To expand our view of this mouse inventor, consider Engelbart's description of how he started on a major computing project (which included development of the mouse) in the early 1950s, while he was working for the predecessor of NASA at the Ames Research Center:

> Graphic vision surges forth of me sitting at a large CRT [cathode ray tube] console, working in ways that are rapidly evolving in front of my eyes (beginning from memories of the radar-screen consoles I used to service). ... [This] evolved within a few days to a general information environment where the basic

concept was a document that would include mixed text and graphic portrayals on the CRT. The imagery carried on to extensions of the symbology and methodology that we humans could employ to do our heavy thinking. There were also images of other people at consoles attached to the same computer complex, simultaneously working in a collaboration mode that would be much closer and more effective than we had ever been able to accomplish.

Within weeks I had committed my career to "augmenting the human intellect."

Engelbart worked at the Stanford Research Institute (SRI) on this project, which did indeed include developing a prototype mouse with his lead engineer Bill English. Around the same time, Telefunken, a company in Germany, independently developed and marketed a mouse of their own, created by turning an already-invented track ball upside-down. Nevertheless, it was thanks to Engelbart's work and his demonstration of the mouse that this became an essential input device, connecting the flat surface of a desk to a computer's planar grid. Engelbart showed off the device and explained how it was used in a stunning demonstration called "the mother of all demos" on December 9, 1968. This was much more than just a chance to put the mouse through its paces. It showed how the mouse worked as part of a system, the oN-Line System (NLS), to enable a wide variety of new capabilities that Engelbart developed over many years in the service of his vision, quoted earlier, of "augmenting human intellect."

To look more thoroughly at the interface level, though, Engelbart's mouse was not meant to be used with an ordinary keyboard, or at least not *only* with such a keyboard. In his demo, Engelbart showed that when he pointed with the mouse, using his right hand, his left hand could move to a chorded keyboard, a five-key device that allowed characters to be input by pressing a combination of keys. The computer user was able to type all the usual glyphs while also operating the mouse. The standard keyboard was retained as part of the interface, available for more rapid text entry when the mouse wasn't being used.

Engelbart's mouse was only one part of an innovative interface system, the component that happened to be adopted. But his input system was also only one innovation in an advanced system for communication and information storage and retrieval. This was the NLS, developed with clear awareness of the Memex as Bush described it in "As We May Think." (In a 1962 report Engelbart quoted at length from this article, and responded to it in detail, considering how it could be practically implemented.) NLS was developed based on this early 1950s idea at Engelbart's lab at SRI, the Augmentation Research Center (ARC), using

Engelbart's signature technique of *bootstrapping*—as parts of the system were developed, they were put to use developing other capabilities.

Engelbart gave his amazing demo in 1968, but earlier, in 1962, he had already prepared an initial, formidable report on the way he was proceeding with the project. This report was titled "Augmenting Human Intellect: A Conceptual Framework." In it, he described the system within which people are able to think, and already effectively augment their thinking, as the H-LAM/T system—the Human augmented by the Language, Artifacts, Methodology plus Training in those three types of augmentation. From this perspective, "Increasing the effectiveness of the individual's use of his basic capabilities is a problem in redesigning the changeable parts," which can have a positive ripple effect through ways of thinking and working. Engelbart was not focused only on the work of the scientist, as Bush was, but also considered that his augmentations to human intellect could offer benefits across practices and disciplines. The first example he gave, in the introduction, was of an architect using augmentation in ways that closely relate to the use of current CAD systems.

Positing that portable electronic reference books could offer important new augmentations and change the way people learn and work together, he wrote, "It seems reasonable to consider the development of automated external symbol manipulation means as a next stage in the evolution of our intellectual power." He continued to develop a detailed cognitive model and to identify where short-term augmentations could have the greatest effect.

In one section of the report, Engelbart introduces a hypothetical individual, Joe, who is a user of an advanced, future augmentation system. While the difference in time in this report is much less than in Bellamy's *Looking Backward*, the essential technique is the same. Engelbart presents a habituated, trained individual of the future who can explain the workings of an unbuilt system—at the personal rather than social level, in this case. Joe argues that for practical reasons—in order to adjust the tools for thinking that are being used—augmented thinkers should know how to program. And for many practical reasons, as well as for better bootstrapping, Engelbart makes the case that the first augmentations for people of any profession should be made to the computer programmer.

This report, still six years away from the famous 1968 demo, already puts the mouse in its place. It is an augmentation particularly useful for someone who types and also needs to indicate a point on the screen—for example, someone who works at drafting and frequently labels part of a drawing, or a copyeditor, or a computer programmer. It isn't a trivial advance, since it conveniently adds a fluid, 2D input to the typed input that computers could easily accept at the time. But it is only one development that comes from application of an extensive conceptual framework, only one step toward a vision of augmented collaborative intellectual work.

Now, let's return to the mouse's public premiere, at the end of 1968, in San Francisco. It's the major conference in computer science and electrical engineering, a joint conference held by the Association for Computing Machinery and the Computer Society of the Institute of Electrical and Electronics Engineers. About four thousand were in the auditorium; among them were leading figures in computing, including Alan Kay (whose work is discussed in chapter 7) and Andries van Dam, whose collaboration with Nelson is described in the next section of this chapter. It's hard to know what everyone in the room was thinking, but Engelbart was not well known at the time and nothing like this demonstration had ever been attempted before. Bill Paxton, the fellow researcher who demonstrated simultaneous text editing with Engelbart in that session, thought that about 90 percent of the computer science community considered him was a "crackpot" and noted that "even we … had trouble understanding what he was doing" (Metz 2008).

The audience's skepticism was met with a demonstration of advanced word processing; the creation, editing, and traversal of hypertext; the collaborative text editing in which Paxton participated; and even real-time videocon-ferencing. Engelbart's interface featured windows—of the sort that were later in widespread use in the Macintosh—allowing him to have several workspaces visible at once. Audience members also saw new and highly effective forms of command input and file system navigation in use. Dynamic file linking and version control may not be the best known of computing concepts, but users who create a desktop shortcut or peek at GitHub to see how a soft-ware project is progressing are involved with them; they too were demonstrated for the first time during this 1968 session. It was van Dam who called this "the mother of all demos." Chuck Thacker, an engineer who was also there, described the typing, mousing Engelbart as "dealing light-ning with both hands."

Engelbart continued his work for decades afterward, including at his Bootstrap Institute at the end of the twen-tieth century. But it's safe to say that his 1968 demo was his greatest, most influential moment.

In describing the vision that inspired him, Engelbart seems to have suggested that all the important aspects of NLS appeared in a flash of insight. His vision was, as his writing makes clear, a strong motivation for his research, but an incomplete view of the solution. Still, Engelbart's initial "graphic vision" was certainly essential to the future-building he undertook. What aspects of it were helpful and worth imitating? Some essential points follow:

• The vision was a personal one, considering a better way of working and thinking. Specifically, Engelbart wrote that it was of "me sitting at a large CRT console, working." The technology isn't imagined by itself, or with regard to abstract capabilities, or even as helping people in general, but within a specific context in which the future-maker is making use of it.

• The system, in this vision, would start by working on a specific object that could be clearly known and discussed, and the "document that would include mixed text and graphic portrayals," but built on this to develop conceptually in new, more general territory: "extensions of the symbology and methodology that we humans could employ to do our heavy thinking."

• The system envisioned would scale up in two important ways. First, as with almost any product, it was easy to imagine many work stations being made so that many individuals would be able to each sit at a system to write, edit, link, and annotate these text-and-graphics documents and what followed them. (Personal computing saw this type of scaling up.) But the vision also scaled from individual to group use, enabling new ways of thinking by connecting individuals and facilitating collaboration. Companies using "information technology" have benefited from this for a while, but massive popular participation in collaborative online projects is more recent, blossoming in the twenty-first century.

Engelbart's 1962 report makes two other points about making the future:

• The future-building takes place on and within a well-developed conceptual framework. Engelbart understood not only existing human abilities for thought, but also the effective ways that intellect is already augmented. He understood where the innovations would be and how their benefits would propagate. He also understood what he wasn't intending to change: As in the H-LAM/T system, he was augmenting (not replacing) a human who was trained in and used language, methodologies, and artifacts. The goal was not to add to or take anything away from this system, but to understand it and develop within it.

• Writing that has science-fictional and utopian aspects is used to describe the vision of the future, what is to be made. This allows for a description that is focused and personal (Joe is described as concretely using augmentations and as having opinions about how people should best do so) but also has advanced into a systematic future, where different advances work together to do more than the sum of their improvements. Joe is not just a guy with a mouse—actually, he uses a light pen instead, but you get

Engelbart understood not only existing human abilities for thought, but also the effective ways that intellect is already augmented. He understood where the innovations would be and how their benefits would propagate.

the point. He is the user of an advanced system, and the way he controls it (he does make use of different, more advanced controls) relates to new capabilities beneath the interface. It also makes sense to say that this part of the report is simply good writing, as Engelbart chose to "show" rather than "tell" what his developments could lead to, following classic advice.

Finally, two points about Engelbart's demo and its lessons for future-building:

• As with his vision, as described in his report, the point is not a single advance, or just a set of individual advances, but the development of a powerful system that allows entirely new ways of working.

• If his 1962 report seemed an example of "show, don't tell," his 1968 demo was a much more literal example of the maxim. Engelbart's speaking about the system, during the ninety-minute presentation, was dramatically connected to his showing how it worked and what it could do. It was a prototype in use, and you could see that NLS hadn't come online only the day before. Engelbart and his collaborators had taken the time to use the system, accommodate themselves to it, and get the training (the T in H-LAM/T) to use it with some effectiveness.

Ted Nelson's Hypertext

Just as many people know only one thing about Douglas Engelbart—that he invented the mouse—there is one best-known fact about Theodor Holm Nelson's accomplishments: He coined the term "hypertext."

He also developed the hypertext concept, by writing about it and implementing systems. He's known for his Project Xanadu, begun in 1960 as the first hypertext project and offering its first released implementation in 2014. He ran one of the few very early retail computer stores that sold the original Apple, or Apple I, computer. He was for a time the editor of the magazine *Creative Computing*, which printed type-in programs and articles. He was the author of highly influential books, with the ones of greatest influence being *Literary Machines* (first published in 1981) and *Computer Lib/Dream Machines* (two books bound as one, back-to-back).[1] He coined more obscure but extremely provocative terms, including "transclusion" (a principle of his hypertext concept), "intertwingled" (the complex interconnected condition of human knowledge), and "teledildonics" (the technological facility for having sex at a distance).

Nelson has offered complex, powerful ideas that helped to build our future; he also speaks and writes incisively to denounce aspects of computer technology that he believes are retrograde. For instance, any computer user now understands "cut and paste" to mean something like "select some text or other media, cause it to disappear from the screen, move the insertion point, and cause it to reappear there." But when a person literally cuts text out of a paper page, moves it to a new location, and pastes it down, for all the material difficulties that might be involved in this process, the text being cut does not ever disappear. The person doing the literal cutting and pasting can see that text or other collage element the whole time, rereading and trying it out in different contexts. For this reason, Nelson has his own special name for what is usually called the cut/copy buffer, the space in memory where a selection is held, unseen. He calls it "the abominable hidey hole." Future-makers are often critical of current technologies; their responses can prompt new designs and new visions.

Nelson has criticism of the World Wide Web, too, but before getting to that, it's best to offer a summary of at least the most important aspects of Nelson's concept of hypertext—and hypermedia, another Nelson coinage— as he laid them out in *Computer Lib/Dream Machines* and *Literary Machines*.

Hypertext for Nelson wasn't just a set of pages where some of the words were blue and underlined, such that clicking on one caused a page to be replaced by another page. In Nelson's view, links of this sort were only one element of hypertext interface, and while they would still have a directionality they would be two-way in an important sense: When you were viewing a particular document, or page, you could see everything that linked to it as well as everything it linked to.

Beyond using links of this sort, a link could take the form of a quotation from the page being linked to. This is called "transclusion." Imagine an extreme case of transclusion: You decide to write a work that consists entirely of quotations from other texts—such as Jonathan Lethem's *Harper's Magazine* essay "The Ecstasy of Influence," David Shields's book *Reality Hunger*, my blog post "Student's Novel Faces Plagiarism Controversy" on *Grand Text Auto* that I did before these two guys wrote their appropriated texts, or Walter Benjamin's *The Arcades Project*. (I admit, that one was written decades before my *Grand Text Auto* post.) The practice of gathering quotations didn't start in the twentieth century, of course; people collected quotes in commonplace books beginning in the fifteenth century. In a system with transclusion, you would select the passages from the texts you are using and they would be included, via linking, from wherever those documents live on the network. A reader could just click to go to the source document, looking at the context in which the quoted passage appears.

A transclusion system was meant to address copyright and royalty issues, since the amount of text or other media that was used in assembling a new document would be precisely known, and the rights owners would be identified. Of course, a document using transclusion wouldn't have to be entirely made of quoted material. New writing could be part of it, and there could be a few block quotations or short quotations; this new writing could then be transcluded by others.

Another way hypertext could work was in the framework of a "stretchtext." A document—imagine it first as all-new writing—could be reduced in size to a short summary or expanded, with sentences and paragraphs changing as the reader zoomed in or out. A stretchtext could have media elements that aren't textual, and of course transclusion could be used in it as well. Indeed, stretchtexts exist today and some are prominent; one of them is the award-winning iPad "app novella" *Pry* by Samantha Gorman and Danny Cannizzaro. However, the stretchtext concept didn't become a general-purpose format, frequently used on a system like the Web. It remains an idea that artists, writers, and programmers employ to create an unusual sort of hypertext.

Nelson worked at Brown University, beginning in 1967, with collaborators on the Hypertext Editing System (HES), an influential early hypertext system and the predecessor to the File Retrieval and Editing System (FRESS). Nelson also describes founding Project Xanadu to create a radical hypertext system in 1960; the project was famous for having no outcome for many decades, although a system (without source code) was finally released in 2014. On the Web, of course. Still, Nelson's influence on hypertext has been due, in large part, to his detailed and rhetorically persuasive descriptions of hypertext in his early books.

The World Wide Web's Formation

As should now be clear, Berners-Lee and his collaborators didn't make up every concept that is the foundation of the Web—they were aware, directly and indirectly, of existing hypertext ideas. The success of the World Wide Web is surely due to two specific factors beyond determination and cleverness:

First, the Web is a simple system, much less powerful than Nelson would like. Not only does it lack built-in support for specific types of hypertext such as stretchtext, it also doesn't even have two-way links. A central registry could provide for such links, as well as transclusion with appropriate payments for authors. But the Web doesn't require any central authority—or, at least, it requires only the hierarchical aspects of the underlying Internet that were already there. The Web would be much less useful without the ultimately centralized Domain Name Service (DNS) that resolves verbal names such as "mit.edu" into numeric addresses. But this system was developed in the

1980s, and predates the Web. Once you can convert your domain names into addresses, your requests only need to route through the Internet to locate a Web server and retrieve information from it. A person who wants to set up a new Web server can just set one up without any interaction with a central registry. In the worst case, dealing with a central authority just means the equivalent of registering a new domain.

Letting people know where that the new server is there is helpful, of course, and in the 1990s a new type of business emerged to help people locate Web resources—including hand-made directories (Yahoo!, Open Directory) and search engines (AltaVista, Google). Such services work to patch up the decentralized Web and allow the discovery of Web resources that would otherwise be obscure. But the Web didn't need to have them in place at the very beginning. They could, and did, grow up afterward. The Web, as it first existed, was a very simple hypertext system. It didn't attempt to solve every problem with an elaborate initial design.

Second, the standards of the Web were offered to everyone rather than being restricted by patents or copyrights. Berners-Lee insisted that the Web not be encumbered, and there are concrete reasons this may have helped the system to succeed. For instance, one of the Web's early competitors, Gopher, offered generally similar ways to traverse hypertext resources online and began gaining traction in 1991. Gopher was more limited in some ways, because of its strongly hierarchical format, but also offered some features that the early Web lacked. While not the only factor that led the Web to prevail, Gopher was dealt a blow in early 1993, when its owner, the University of Minnesota, said that it would charge to license its Gopher server, the dominant one. The choice in the early 1990s between a clearly free and open technology and one that might face further restrictions helped to make one of them—the Web—look like a better choice.

As I mentioned, hypertext pioneer Ted Nelson isn't a full-on fan of the World Wide Web, even though this famous system has broadened access to some forms of hypertext. He writes, "Trying to fix HTML is like trying to graft arms and legs onto hamburger. ... EMBEDDED MARKUP IS A CANCER." He continues, "HTML is precisely what we were trying to PREVENT—ever-breaking links, links going outward only, quotes you can't follow to their origins, no version management, no rights management."[2] Without knowing about Nelson's contributions to hypertext and computing, this may seem like pure negativity; if one knows just a little about history, it may seem like sour grapes. I tend to think that this perspective comes from a different view of what the future could have been. It has particular virtues, but was also complex, more difficult to implement, and required a centralized system for rights management. On the one hand, a wider array of features didn't mean, by itself, that Nelson's system was better. On the other hand, the Web, however successful it has been, is not beyond critique.

As far as future-making is concerned, these are the two, clear lessons from the early success of the Web:

• The right level of simplicity/complexity is important, even if it means removing some of the features of a vision, and of a systematic future, that other future-makers really love. A vision has to be understood and accepted, and one that is too complex to understand or implement has little chance.

• Openness, an ability to be shared, and freedom to study and build on a system are really important to whether or not people choose to adopt and further develop new ideas and systems.

THE COMPUTER BECOMES A BOOK

The development of the notebook computer offers numerous future-making lessons. The initial concept was quite ambitious and far out, but not too far out—important aspects could be accomplished, while much was still left to strive for. The idea was based on an educational philosophy, was human centered and formed with people's activities and thinking in mind, and was developed with an awareness of important precomputer technologies for thinking, such as paper notebooks. The people developing the vision, and the main person who framed it, acknowledged that the project would have an influence on how people did intellectual work. They looked for signs of their work's influence and strove to make it positive.

Just as one important digital media imagination was of the hypertextual network, another, related to it and compatible with it, was that of a computer that is personal, portable, and open to exploration and experimentation. This concept of a book-like computer, a notebook computer, is largely due to Alan Kay, who called the system he imagined a Dynabook.[1]

People often view new media pioneers as seers, uncannily accurate predictors of the future. This is a way of revering these innovators, but it doesn't capture everything about their role as future-makers. Alan Kay has been described (even by me) as having "foretold" the current state of notebook computing. But Kay and his collaborators didn't really foretell it—they made the future we now live in, one in which we have computers as ready to hand, and as well designed, as books.

In the 1950s the computer was conceptualized by many experts as a building-sized "giant brain." Today, while we have rack-mounted units, boxes made to sit on or under desks, and tiny embedded systems, when someone speaks of a computer, and particularly of "my computer," they often mean something the size, shape, and heft of a book. While people seldom shelve their notebook computers with paper notebooks and other hardbacks, the metaphor of the computer as book has been a powerful one in reframing the way we think about computation and the purposes to which it can be put.

Other important technologies we frequently encounter have changed in scale and situation to some extent. The airplanes most people fly on are significantly larger than the first one put together by those bicycle-builders, the Wright Brothers, and they're also enclosed, made of different materials, propelled differently, and part of a network of regulation, of the architectural and organizational systems of airports, and of industry. Other transportation technologies have changed less in the same time, but may be on the brink of significant change. If people have their cars driven by Google's corporate computing power, rather than by human drivers, our relationship to the automobile could certainly be transformed. But at this point, transportation and mobility technologies haven't been reshaped to the extent that general-purpose computing has been.

Batch and Time-Sharing

To understand the transformations of computing, and the idea of personal computing specifically, it is useful to consider the two eras that preceded personal computing: The batch era, corresponding to mainframe computing, and the time-sharing era, in which the minicomputer was emblematic. All three computing paradigms (batch, time-sharing, and personal computing) overlap in various ways. There are still mainframe computers in use today, for instance, and we have "batch jobs" that run on today's personal computers. These three paradigms nevertheless represent different practices that predominated during the history of computing, shaping the way people thought about computing and imagined its possibilities. As computer use moved through these phases, anxieties about what computing would bring, and hopes for its future, also shifted.

The main concept in batch processing was grouping similar types of work together and doing it all at once. This means breaking down tasks so that the components of a task can all be done together, as with grading everyone's first exam question before moving on to the next one. To "batch" work together in this way wasn't an idea original to a certain type of computer, or to digital computing at all. Decades earlier, work was structured like this, as Martin Campbell-Kelly and William Aspray explain: "The reason for this largely manual enterprise—it could have been run on almost identical lines in the 1890s—was that all existing data-processing technologies, whether punched-card machines or computers, operated in what was known as batch-processing mode. Transactions were first batched in hundreds or thousands, then sorted, then processed, and finally totaled, checked, and dispatched."[2] It wasn't only business processes that were done in batches, but also the computation of tables for various purposes: scientific, or in some cases military—for example, the firing tables that the famous early computer ENIAC, developed at the University of Pennsylvania, first computed. Rather than see batch processing as an outcome of the main-frame computer, it's more sensible to see the development of the mainframe as prompted by this batch mode of working.

Programming in the batch era was an unforgiving, bureaucratic process that required the programmer to more or less fully plan and complete work beforehand. Programmers needed to write programs and use a key-punch machine (or have someone else use a keypunch machine on their behalf) to prepare a deck of punched cards, which would then be taken to the window of the room where the mainframe was located. After handing the cards over to priestly attendants, the programmer would need to wait for the submitted job to have its turn; the output would then be provided on paper. An error of a single character would still require use of the keypunch machine to correct, and might require the programmer to wait several more hours, since access to the computer was regulated.

A major new aspect of interactive computing was that a single computer served a large number of users, typing and reading at terminals, all at once. In a way, the concept of the batch process was similar—one would get a set of punched-card stacks and run them one after the other. But interactive computing transformed this process so that people could write and edit programs while actually using the computer, rather than writing code in pencil and having it keypunched in. Essentially, the programmer was no longer waiting on the machine; the machine was waiting on the programmer.

Time-sharing was the era in which BASIC was developed, although many know the language from microcomputers. Unlike COBOL and Fortran, which were designed for punched cards, BASIC was one of the languages made for interactive use—so that programs could be typed, tried out, and revised. BASIC, with its origins in time-sharing, also became the lingua franca of the home computer era.[3]

While time-sharing brought many benefits, computing pioneers saw an opportunity for further ways that digital media could extend and amplify human thought and better serve people. The ideas of personal computing, present in some respects by the end of World War II in Vannevar Bush's vision of the Memex, were essential to Alan Kay's computer-as-book concept. With this sketch of the first two important eras in computing history, batch processing and time-sharing, we are ready to move to consider Kay's vision, a powerful formulation of the idea of personal computing.

The Dynabook's Conceptual Innovations

At the risk of reducing Kay's important invention to a manifesto, let's consider a few influential concepts of the

Dynabook. It was for everyone, was personal and owned by the user, was portable, was a metamedium, and supported truly personal and reflective work.

An important idea about computing expressed in the Dynabook is that it is for "children of all ages," not specifically experts, researchers, businesspeople, or the like. Perhaps this system wasn't truly for everyone, since it wasn't an instrumental, single-purpose tool for those interested only in tool use, but it was for all those willing to make play part of their computing practice.

Kay conceptualized the Dynabook as a general-purpose computer that the user would own: "What then is a personal computer? One would hope that it would be both medium for containing and expressing arbitrary symbolic notions, and also a collection of useful tools for manipulating these structures, with ways to add new tools to the repertoire. ... 'Personal' also means owned by its user."[4]

In retrospect, that's exactly what a personal computer is, but this was not an obvious plan for computing at the beginning of the 1970s. As described, another computing revolution had recently taken hold, supplanting the batch-mode system of cards, keypunch machines, climate-controlled mainframes, and operators and machines running indifferently on schedules. Instead of waiting on the computer, the computer waited on the programmer, slicing up its time between many people at different terminals. Interactive programming—changing a program

An important idea about computing expressed in the Dynabook is that it is for "children of all ages," not specifically experts, researchers, businesspeople, or the like.

on the fly to fix a bug or experiment with a different approach—finally became practical, and a great advance was made over the first way the practice of programming had been conducted.

In formulating the Dynabook, Kay saw that his demanding users and programmers—young children were his initial focus, although he imagined the system being used by all—would need more power than time-sharing systems could provide if they were to truly use the computer to do general-purpose programming. It would also be necessary to take full advantage of the computer's ability as a metamedium, its capability for simulating other media. As Kay wrote, "This means that we should either build a new resource several hundred times the capacity of current machines and share it (very difficult and expensive), or we should investigate the possibility of giving each person his own powerful machine. We chose the second approach."[5] Even if it was less difficult and expensive, it didn't prove possible to pack the capabilities Kay had specified into a form like today's notebook computer or tablet. They could be realized on a desktop computer, an "interim Dynabook," however, and they were. The system's workings were developed in this sort of personal form. While that meant setting aside the goal of portability, increasing miniaturization of course eventually brought that within reach.

The computer, as Dynabook, is not just a processor of information, but a medium, and indeed a *metamedium*, one that can serve as all other media:

> The essence of a medium is very much dependent on the way messages are embedded, changed, and viewed. Although digital computers were originally designed to do arithmetic computation, the ability to simulate the details of any descriptive model means that the computer, viewed as a medium itself, can be all other media if the embedding and viewing methods are sufficiently well provided. Moreover, this new "metamedium" is active—it can respond to queries and experiments.[6]

Furthermore, the Dynabook is not just for communication and information access, but for personal reflection: "Although it can be used to communicate with others through the 'knowledge utilities' of the future such as a school 'library' (or business information system), we think that a large fraction of its use will involve reflexive communication of the owner with himself through this personal medium, much as paper and notebooks are currently used."[7] Although there may be elements of this sort of personal use in the Memex concept, Kay turned things around so that what we normally consider the expertise and purpose of computers (information access) is deemphasized in favor of reflection.

Among other things, the Dynabook reframed the purpose of the computer in humanistic terms. It was understood as being for learning, exploration, "creative thought," reflexive writing, and communication with one's self as well as with others.

Smalltalk, the GUI, and the Dynabook in Use

The unusual status of the Dynabook makes it difficult to understand historically. In part, it was the plan used over decades to develop the notebook computer and the tablet—the important hardware aspects of the project were realized by many others. It was a vision for flexible, educational engagement with computing that continues to this day. And, it was a working software system, featuring the graphical user interface (GUI) in largely the same form it is used today and offering the capabilities of object-oriented programming via Smalltalk.

Was the Dynabook "unrealized," as people often write of it? The answer is yes, no, no, and no. First, the full vision of the project as a system for learning, within culture and society, has indeed never been completely realized in the form of a particular product. Second, the most fundamental aspect of the project—personal computing—was

Among other things, the Dynabook reframed the purpose of the computer in humanistic terms. It was understood as being for learning, exploration, "creative thought," reflexive writing, and communication with one's self as well as with others.

realized in important ways back in the 1970s. Third, the core software of the project was also realized—it was developed by Kay and his collaborators. And, finally, fourth, the essential hardware was realized too, over a longer time span, and by many others working in different contexts, although Kay was also involved in this development.

Having looked at the Dynabook at a high level, it's now important to dig into some details and see how the early software, running on the interim Dynabook, worked. The Dynabook is a powerful idea, but also was a technological system with working components. Children did use the interim Dynabook to program, learn, and create. And from looking at this history, we can see how the future that we're living in—the era of personal computing and notebook computing—was built.

The Dynabook was given that name in 1972, but Kay had started work on a portable computer at Xerox PARC in 1970. It was called "KiddiKomp," and was based on an earlier concept of Kay's, from 1968. While the sort of book-sized computer that Kay envisioned wasn't made in the 1970s, there was a first approximation to the Dynabook made in prototype by Xerox in 1978, a computer called the NoteTaker. It weighed almost fifty pounds, but, as it ran on battery power, could be taken aboard a plane and used in flight—indeed, it was. While only ten were made, the computer served to inspire mass-manufactured systems such as the Osborne 1. Xerox's portable system ran Smalltalk.

The two software contributions that stand out from Kay's Dynabook research are Smalltalk (an operating system and programming language that developed many of the principles of object-oriented programming) and the graphical user interface. Both of these existed in an early form in Ivan Sutherland's Sketchpad, as Kay often points out. The programming language SIMULA, another precedent, provided a more refined object-oriented language. Kay's contributions were critical to developing these computing concepts, which still serve many purposes today. As the interim Dynabook was being developed, the main purpose it served was play, exploration, and user-directed learning.

Smalltalk had children as users beginning in 1973, when Adele Goldberg joined Kay from Stanford University and began to teach children how to program in the language. Early on, the children programmed not only animations and demos, but also complete tools for drawing, illustration, music, and circuit design—these developed by twelve-year-olds and fifteen-year-olds. Kay and his collaborators did have trouble extending the project beyond a talented few from Palo Alto schools, but it was remarkable that Smalltalk was used so effectively by a group of young users.[8] The language wasn't only useful for children. Eventually, Smalltalk had a successful commercial life on

Wall Street, where programmers found it good for rapidly developing interfaces for traders. Smalltalk is still commercially available, and Kay developed a new implementation of the language, Squeak, beginning in 1996. Squeak, in turn, was developed to include the Etoys framework and made part of the One Laptop Per Child project, which is discussed later in this chapter.

Personal and Portable Computing

Alan Kay begins a 1993 article on the history of Smalltalk with this text, which refers to his commercial notebook computer (not the Xerox Alto) as a more recent "Interim Dynabook":

> I'm writing this introduction in an airplane at 35,000 feet. On my lap is a five pound notebook computer—1992's "Interim Dynabook"—by the end of the year it sold for under $700. It has a flat, crisp, high-resolution bitmap screen, overlapping windows, icons, a pointing device, considerable storage and computing capacity, and its best software is object-oriented. It has advanced networking built-in and there are already options for wireless networking. Smalltalk runs on this system, and is one of the main systems I use for my current work

with children. In some ways this is more than a Dynabook (quantitatively), and some ways not quite there yet (qualitatively). All in all, pretty much what was in mind during the late sixties.[9]

Head back to your seat from the rear of an airplane today and you are likely to see modern-day Dynabook users undertaking a few different tasks: Watching movies, modifying spreadsheets, building PowerPoint decks, and perhaps (when in-flight Wi-Fi is installed and working) answering emails and browsing the Web. It's less likely that someone will be exploring a complex simulation, unless it's in form of a video game. Those watching movies—and there are likely to be many doing so, on seat-back computers or on their notebook computers—are engaged in a very standard type of media consumption, one that isn't really part of the Dynabook vision. Those people working with spreadsheets may be doing important computational exploration, but they are using a method of calculating values that is now rather antiquated. The people preparing presentations are getting ready to use their computers to aid communication and collaboration, but almost always rely on the "slide" format rather than some more flexible and powerful means of multimedia support.

The interim Dynabooks we have today have developed in fits and starts, offering new ways of working that then seem to more or less solidify for decades. Our notebook computers have become essential business tools in almost every industry. It's less certain that they are suitable for children of all ages, people who want to use them to explore computation and to explore how computation can be used to model and question the world. But there has been other development work focused on young computer users, work that strives to build the future imagined in the original Dynabook concept.

One Laptop Per Child and the XO

If we're looking to find the most Dynabook-like computer that has been mass produced, there would be a few reasonable candidates. Looking beyond the standard range of notebook computers, the iPad presents itself as one possibility. In terms of software and hardware—and the co-development of these by Apple—the system does exhibit many features of the Dynabook, and has a similar form factor to the original Dynabook model. Several qualities of iOS and the iPad seem quite evidently opposed to the ideals of the Dynabook, though. The iPad is optimized for media consumption and the purchase of apps, which users cannot easily make or freely share. Specifically, while a user is allowed to develop an app, such a program cannot directly be given away. *If* Apple approves it via a process designed for professionals, the user may choose to sell the program through Apple's marketplace; the price, if one gets this approval, can be set to $0. Essentially, this system—however slick and well-designed—has been constructed first and foremost for corporate enrichment, not personal enrichment, play, exploration, and sharing, and certainly not activity (beyond media consumption) being undertaken by children.

However amazing a product, the openness to imagination and creativity (an aspect that allows people to better participate in future-making of their own) is lacking in Apple's Dynabook-like tablet offerings. One could ask if there are any systems designed with different principles. There are, and for several reasons. Computers and software made by companies, who of course seek to earn profits, do not always emphasize media consumption or place restrictions on sharing programs. Whether you use OS X, Windows, or GNU/Linux, you are free to write programs and give them away to people online. The recipients may get a warning about how it's dangerous to download and run software, but programs can still be freely shared today.

Another reason: Some computer systems are developed in other ways. One of them was the XO, developed by Nicholas Negroponte's educational nonprofit One Laptop Per Child (OLPC) beginning in 2005. (OLPC did other hardware development work, but I will focus on their first computer.) The project was motivated by Seymour Papert's constructionist ideas and his use of computers for learning. Not only was the Dynabook an important inspiration for the development of the XO; Kay—who was influenced by Papert early in his work—also collaborated on the development of this computer. The XO included a version of Smalltalk, Squeak Etoys.

The idea presented in the title of the One Laptop Per Child project is that young people, even in the poorest areas of the world, should have access to their own computer to facilitate their learning and exploration. It's not enough to put one computer in a classroom with dozens of students: The best system for learning will be always available for a child's use—and will provide opportunities for collaboration, via the network. Because these computers were made for use throughout the world, they were developed to be rugged, to require little power, and to have multilingual keyboards and interfaces. The idea was to have governments purchase and distribute them, and coordinate their support along with teacher training. While the centerpiece of OLPC was certainly the XO computer that it developed, the organization was always imagined as an educational effort, rather than one based on technology.

The concept that became the XO was unveiled as "the $100 Laptop," although the price of the original computer ended up being almost twice that. This and other aspects of the project provided some grist for those who wanted to find fault with OLPC. Some countries signed on, only to retract their interest later. The project was initially dismissed by Bill Gates and Intel Chairman Craig Barrett. When Microsoft and, briefly, Intel later allied with OLPC to offer a version of Windows on the original hardware, some saw the project as abandoning its free-software ideals. The exclusive environment the laptop used had been the free and open Sugar, running on GNU/Linux and developed for OLPC. As might have been expected, deployments of laptops and interactions with governments did not always go smoothly. The in-house technology development work of OLPC was focused on the first laptop; the project continues to support these laptops and manage additional sales through an office in Miami.[10]

While the project was not without problems, it would be hard to claim that OLPC wasn't successful in some ways. The organization shipped 2.5 million XO computers for children around the world, with Uruguay becoming the first country to provide a laptop for every child. In years after the initial development of the XO, OLPC focused on the poorest and least literate countries, showing the broad applicability of its approach to personal computing to education. And, even before Intel became involved in the OLPC project, and despite Intel's initial disparagement of OLPC, the company responded by offering what is generally seen as a direct competitor to the XO, a low-cost netbook specifically targeted for the developing world, the

Intel Classmate. While OLPC hasn't reached every child, it did have a direct and indirect effect of getting computing to millions of children.

The Dynabook and Future-Making

The difficulty in declaring whether the Dynabook project was realized and to what extent it was completed is, in terms of future-making, better thought of as a feature than a bug. If the Dynabook could be reduced to a single, very specific innovation, such as the overlapping windows of a graphical interface, it would be easier to declare it fully realized, but much harder to see the overall cultural importance. If it were just a high-level idea with no specific plan for implementation, there would be no specifics to consider. Such an idea would be much easier to dismiss; even if the vision appealed to us, it would be hard to figure out where to get started developing it. Here are a few aspects of the Dynabook that contributed to its effective future-making:

• It is human-centered, based on the types of use and activity it is meant to enables. The Dynabook can be thought of as a particular device, but it is more a constellation of new ways of working and thinking, socially situated, than a widget or gadget.

• It is based on principles and philosophies, educational ones, in this case. Its design flows from those principles.

• It was planned to have aspects (such as portability in a tablet-like form factor) which were not completely beyond reach, but would take decades to fully develop. The concept and the way it related to human uses of technology encouraged this development.

• It had other aspects that could be and were realized in software over the course of a few years.

• It is based on empowering metaphors of information systems that are personal and serve humanistic purposes (the book, the notebook).

• It recognizes that computing can influence cultural activity positively or negatively, without assuming that the Dynabook will determine culture or be "just a tool" that is culturally neutral. The concept and project take responsibility for the ways in which they may change computer use and education.

Alan Kay has recently noted that a few prominent systems, such as the Microsoft Surface, now come with both a stylus and a keyboard, as his original Dynabook concept did, and that it took a very long time for the industry to see the importance of both interfaces. There is something to be said for flexibility and openness to different styles of use, but this comment about the stylus seems to me—pardon the pun—to put too fine of a point on it. For instance, the configuration of portable computers that has become pervasive is the clamshell arrangement in which the screen folds down over the keyboard like a book closing. My own computer—my 2017 interim Dynabook—is of this sort, and I have used one like it for many years.

Whether this more book-like chassis is inherently better than the more tablet-like arrangement of the Dynabook, which is also well represented in computing today, is worth considering, but does not seem to be a really central issue for the Dynabook vision and for tracing its influence. My ability to use the system reflectively, for instance, to take notes, arrange reading that interests me, and communicate with myself as well as others, is a powerful connection to the Dynabook vision and means more than the presence or absence of a hinge or a stylus. And, as far as future-making is concerned, the general features of the Dynabook concept and project are what seem particularly compelling. We don't have to appeal to the Microsoft Surface to understand the power of this way of thinking. Kay has shown, regardless of interface specifics, how six important ways of thinking can allow one to engage in future-making when developing a vision that involves new technologies.

CURRENT FICTIONS: DESIGN FICTION, SCIENCE FICTION

At some of the extremes of powerful writing, representing some of the richest imagination of the future, there are a few things to be learned about the practice of future-making. One is that being radical and different is not, by itself, what makes visions of these sorts compelling—they work because they are connected to everyday, known re-alities and the social world we currently inhabit. Another is that, however important human-centered design is, it's possible to productively start thinking about the future from the standpoint of specific materials and technolo-gies. Finally, we can have positive or negative ideas about the future, and about the implications of our technological developments, and all of these ideas can be valuable.

The term "design fiction" only dropped in 2005 in Bruce Sterling's book *Shaping Things* and was first treated in detail in 2009. It refers to a speculative, imaginative practice, which might be expressed in writing, video, live demos, prototype objects, or in other ways. Design fiction is explicitly involved with exploring the future, and with ways to better live in society and culture. The focus is not on coming up with solutions to today's problems using today's technologies, materials, and social configurations, but on looking ahead.

Developing design fiction may take the form of writing or video production, but it is essentially a design practice, even if undertaken by thinkers without formal training as designers. So it makes sense to begin by understanding what characterizes design and what the status of design is in our culture.

Here's a concise definition of design by one of the most famous American designers, Charles Eames, given in a 1972 interview which the Eames office made into a film: "One could describe design as a plan for arranging elements to accomplish a particular purpose."[1] This remains an important definition; for instance, it was quoted by Julian Bleecker in his foundational work.[2]

Without getting into the details of different design processes, designers address purposes and solve problems. They do not always do so by producing a new object of the expected sort, ready to replace an old one. For instance, a standing desk may solve the problem that typically calls for a better chair without any new chair design being part of the solution.

It is a mark of quality for something to be designed or made by a designer, as with designer jeans and furniture. Of course jeans that aren't designer jeans were also designed, but we don't believe them to be designed as carefully, intentionally, and expertly. Design is concerned with how these jeans look, and how stylish they are, as well as how they feel to wear, just as an architect is concerned with how usable and inhabitable a building is as well as how it looks from various vantage points.

Design is certainly considered better than a lack of design, but what about the relationship between art and design? There are prominent people, including artist/ designer John Maeda, Head of Design and Inclusion at Automattic, who do not spend much time distinguishing between art and design. But many people, including those who work as designers, artists, or in some cases both, do distinguish the practices. Eames's second answer in his interview is to the question "Is design an expression of art?" to which he replies, "I would rather say it's an expression of purpose. It may, if it is good enough, later be judged as art."[3]

Artists do not have clients to whom they are accountable in the same way that designers do—although of course gallery owners, curators, collectors, and those awarding commissions do fulfill somewhat similar roles. Perhaps a better articulation of the difference is that, as Eames says, designers work to solve preexisting problems and toward preexisting purposes, whether they are creating a functional and visually pleasing teapot or communicating a message effectively on a poster. While the Museum of Modern Art in New York has a prominent design collection and they and many other galleries and museums now display design objects alongside so-called "fine art" works, making art is certainly widely considered the higher-status practice in the United States and globally, and is venerated in many contexts.

Without trying to fully define what fiction is, the relevant aspects of it for the concept of design fiction are that it is a systematic imagination. Someone writing a fiction has to somehow have in mind a fictional world, corresponding to ours in some way and different in other ways, that is developed through imagination. Since design is also systematic and not isolated to a particular chair or other object, there is actually a rather obvious connection between the development of fictions and the process of design.

We could expect, then, design fiction to be more focused toward purposes and problem-solving than fiction is generally. Design fiction also makes the important connection between the systematic thinking of both design and fiction. This is a reasonable way to distinguish design fiction from the utopian writing of Edward Bellamy. *Looking Backward* provided a compelling and important view of a better society, but Bellamy did not realize his speculative society in as fully systematic a way as a practicing designer would, demonstrating how this society was designed, and how its problems had been solved, in detail. This is one reason the initial appeal of his ideas may not have been longer lasting.

If there were such a thing as "art fiction" that attempted some of the aspects of design fiction without the attention toward a particular purpose, it would be differently focused than design fiction, proposing visions and impulses rather than specific rearrangements of elements that allow for new types of social life.

I believe the Futurists were involved in this sort of future-directed, but more diffuse and less specifically directed, art fiction. Their excitement about technology, industrialization, and war was made manifest in their writings and in other forms of art, and was coherent and systematic in some ways. Also, they did embrace the technological media systems that were consistent with their attitudes. But technology simply exhilarated them; they did not distinguish between any types that could be better or worse for particular people or purposes. They did not propose to develop technology in particular new ways in their work; they simply celebrated how it hurtled toward them.

Design Fiction on Video

Design fictions can be in any medium, and some of the most famous have been presented as videos. A standout corporate production of this sort is the 2011 video *A Day Made of Glass*, which lasts five and a half minutes and was followed up by a series of videos, all created by glass manufacturer Corning, Inc.[4] By early 2017, the video had been viewed more than twenty-six million times, more than five times as many views as the original Futurama exhibit garnered.

The video depicts glass surfaces of different sorts that can serve as digital displays and, in a few cases, can also darken to block out light. By showing a day in the life of a couple, which uses glass computer interfaces extensively, it proposes a future in which people are free to move their computing-based work and media, currently tied to particular devices, freely between surfaces.

In the video, the interface to everything becomes visual and involves touching glass. Even a woman's search for clothing, at a store where she would typically be able to feel the different garments when first looking though them, is conducted through a glass interface, through the navigation of menus. The woman is also greeted by name by a *Minority Report*–like system (my reference is to the 2002 film], from almost a decade beforehand, which recognizes her as she arrives to look for clothing. In this video, unlike in the earlier movie, the recognition of the customer is treated without irony.

Of course, there are never fingerprints or smudges on any of the glass surfaces. They serve both as the surfaces of furnishings and as fluid interfaces. At the end of the video, we see that the traditional paper book has replaced with a glass ebook reader, although the couple's bedroom still has a few nonglass items, such as three paintings. Some say that when your only tool is a hammer, everything looks like a nail. When your only product is glass, it seems that every problem can be solved by this product. In Corning's video, the glass is more than half full.

While every aspect of *A Day Made of Glass* may not end up defining our future, it's worth noting what Corning has done well and what contributed to the successful reception of this video. The video is a slick production, of course. The company shows how Corning products will be integrated into many aspects of life—work, communication with family and coworkers, and leisure time—and how people of different ages will interact differently. (One of the girls in the family selects and resizes a virtual photo on the refrigerator and playfully draws on it, for example.) The video shows glass functioning in standard and well-known ways, regulating light, keeping the elements out, providing the structure of a countertop or table. And, of course, it extends the role of the material into new sorts of more pervasive computer display and interface. While the vision is striking, then, it isn't truly radical in that it does not require that we revise our notions of daily life or of computing. Rather, it extends existing facilities for work, shopping, and home life beyond what we typically imagine.

The same could be said about the Futurama exhibits and about Bellamy's utopian Boston, but *A Day Made of Glass* makes the case, dare I say, clear:

• Powerful new aspects of the future are all the more persuasive when situated in existing, familiar experiences that we value and want to preserve.

Beyond this, there's a point that resonates with Bel Geddes's Futurama:

• Productive visions of the future can start from imagining the properties of new materials, or from thinking about what a corporation can accomplish. Arising from a commercial context, or the context of a celebrated avant-garde art movement, doesn't make a future concept right or wrong, useless or effective, by itself.

When the Glass Is Dark

In Paul's First Epistle to the Corinthians, during a discussion of love, he briefly mentions not being able to see as well

Powerful new aspects of the future are all the more persuasive when situated in existing, familiar experiences that we value and want to preserve.

as we later will: "For now we see through a glass, darkly," as it is rendered in the most influential English translation, the King James Bible. While the passage is about an encounter with the divine, to some it recalls Plato's allegory of the cave and the way that people in that imagined environment saw shadows rather than reality. To others it evokes the difficulty of seeing the future. The phrase has been used directly or in altered form as the title of many works dealing with the future, usually in dystopian ways. Among these are Philip K. Dick's *A Scanner, Darkly*, a 1977 science fiction novel with autobiographical aspects that was made into a 2006 animated (and rotoscoped) film by Richard Linklater. In it, there are several things that are difficult to see: a confusion of identities produced by a "scramble suit" that makes the protagonist look like many different people in rapid succession, for instance, and the matter of who is undercover and working for the police. Besides the many references to this phrase, more than a dozen literary and musical works, and almost as many TV episodes, use the phrase "through a glass, darkly" as their title directly.

Scholars seeking to understand what type of "glass" is meant in this verse have looked through the dark glass of ancient writing and determined that it is probably a mirror, and several recent translations of the bible use the term. So, one reason we might be looking through a glass darkly would be because we are looking at a black mirror, for instance, such as the mirror-like surface of our mobile phone when it is turned off, or sleeping.

The television program *Black Mirror* is an anthology science fiction series, similar in format to *The Twilight Zone*. Each episode is its own story with its own cast, the themes and genre of the series providing the only connection between them. The format is an old one, and a somewhat antiquated one, extending back to the golden age of radio in the 1920s. Few recent TV shows have used the anthology format; one of the other shows that has is *Fargo*, a crime comedy series, similarly dark, which is based on the Coen Brothers' film. But the anthology format is, for the most part, a throwback.

While the format is a retro aspect of *Black Mirror*, the episodes are united in being set in the future, a near future with recognizable contemporary technologies such as the smartphone, social networks, and virtual reality taking a prominent place—an exaggerated place, that makes for a satirical result. *Black Mirror* generally presents stories, and worlds, that can be understood as dystopian. They are a type of no-place, a species of utopia, which offers an example of how bad things can get if we let our worst habits and practices continue to grow, and if we continue to develop and use technology uncritically. A few of the episodes do not have the horrifically negative endings that typify the series, but these episodes, too, are involved with questioning technology and exploring its consequences through presenting a world that does not exist, at least, not yet.

To concretely discuss the image of ourselves that *Black Mirror* provides, and how the series works to do this, I'll focus on the first episode released after Netflix took over the series. (The first seven episodes, produced 2011–2014, were done in the United Kingdom by Channel 4.) I'm going to give away the ending to this episode, which is about a world in which everyone is getting upvoted and downvoted by others all the time, and in which a person's status and even their essential personal liberty depend on their rating. If you notice the title of the episode when you start watching it—"Nosedive"—you will pretty much be spoiled already. Perhaps the biggest surprise is that tone of the episode is not as extremely grim as most of the other episodes in the series—the main character ends up humiliated and incarcerated, but is not, for instance, recycled into an energy drink. The ending offers more humor than despair.

The premise of the episode is that everyone, including of course the main character, Lacie Pound, has a rating between one and five that results from other people giving them some number of stars, via mobile phone, either when they encounter them "in real life" or after other interactions. Obviously the ability to indicate ratings in this way is not science-fictional. In fact, a version of the app

Peeple, which allows people to rate other people (not just products, restaurants, or films) in exactly this way was released in March 2016. The system depicted in "Nosedive" further relies on general-purpose face recognition to indicate who is being rated. While this would currently be hard to do quickly using only a phone's computing power, it could certainly be done on a server: commercial software to identify people by their faces is already in place at border crossings, casinos, and even megachurches. So, the plausibility of the basic technology in this episode is pretty much 100 percent—I give it five stars.

During the episode, many characters are involved in service interactions with Lacie, and they tend to act in artificial, extremely polite ways. This is hardly dystopian; it is at most a gentle satire on the systems that society has already set up to compel pleasantness. Lacie seeks upward social mobility and wishes to move into a new house in a neighborhood that is restricted to those of higher status. Again, given the existing barriers of income and getting approved for a mortgage, this situation seems only slightly exaggerated, or shifted so that it is captured by a new, explicit quantitative measure. The twist, however, as the title suggests, is that a few negative interactions in a row can cause a person's rating to plummet, excluding them from benefits that seemed ordinary beforehand. Lacie finds this out the hard way. She also discerns that even those who are rated very highly (such as a childhood friend who extends, then retracts an invitation to be her maid of honor) appear to spend a large amount of time and effort cultivating their high rating.

One of the usual things about "Nosedive" is that it has an ending that, while certainly negative, is rather comedic. Lacie ends up jailed in a glassy cell opposite another person, a man, who is also well dressed but seems to have fallen on hard times and low ratings. With nothing to lose, they end up yelling insults at each other in a rather exuberant way, seemingly pleased that they get to vent but perhaps also that no one is hurt, physically or in terms of their ratings.

The episode shows us that technology is not always directly to blame, and it may mainly intensify the problematic social urges we already have. Quantitative social ratings may magnify our existing difficulties, but it's ultimately our being jerks to each other that is the problem. We can imagine the people portrayed in the episode being emotionally hurt and contriving to socially disadvantage others, or attempting to socially advantage themselves, without this rating system being in place. The real statement of the episode is that the social world and the technological world are deeply intertwined, or, as Ted Nelson would say, intertwingled. Perhaps it's also appropriate that in the episode Lacie speaks to her brother and, remotely, to her childhood friend from her kitchen of the future, where the social and technological mix.

Early on, I mentioned the future-building potential of another science fiction show, *Star Trek*. Interesting, perhaps, that the most mirror-like episode ("Mirror, Mirror") presents a view both of the utopian world of the usual *Star Trek* and of its opposite, an empire dedicated to war that has a similar *Enterprise* and similar crew members on it. To make decisions about our collective future, it's helpful to know what can go wrong as well as what can be right. The lessons for future-making, then, are as follows:

• Showing how a negative future can arise can still be helpful, and can provoke a critical response to current technological development.

• Richly imagining how the social world interacts with technology is always important, whether one wishes to show a better, cheerful future (as Corning did) or warn us about a dangerous, negative possibility (as *Black Mirror* does).

CONCLUSION:
PRACTICES FOR FUTURE-MAKING

I wrote this book mostly during 2016. One of the many famous, beloved people who died during this year was the Canadian singer and songwriter Leonard Cohen. Perhaps a statement from his song "The Future" sounds more appropriate these days than Alan Kay's optimistic statement, which I used as the book's epigraph. As Cohen put it, "I've seen the future, brother: it is murder."

It's impossible to look at positive, productive visions of the future without seeing the contexts of despair out of which they arise or into which they sink. The better world of the original General Motors Futurama exhibit was presented just before the onset of World War II. Vannevar Bush's vision of a better system for research, scholarship, and the promotion of knowledge was forged in the fires of that war, and specifically the fires of the Manhattan

Project. A delighted public experienced the second Futurama at the 1964 New York World's Fair, at the same time President Johnson was taking the country deeper into the Vietnam War. If we waited until the outlook was completely sunny to try to build a future for ourselves, we would never make the attempt.

So it still seems appropriate to me, from this current perspective of 2017, to think seriously about how to build a better future. While the present looks more dire, to me and to many of us, than it did a year ago, the future is still unwritten. There is still space and time to imagine it and pursue it intentionally, to actively construct better social opportunities and a better built environment. In the interest of encouraging this imagination, even as some seek to drive us into the past, I have provided this consideration of the future and how we can make it together.

To close, then, a few summary comments about future-making that touch on some of the most effective principles and approaches:

What formats or media should be used when developing a new future? Embrace the ones that you celebrate in the "content" of your future vision. Work across categories of art, design, writing, and media-making. Use the detail of overlooked media forms to test and refine your vision. Perhaps the best format is a working version of one's system, a demo or prototype. Nevertheless, imagining how

It's impossible to look at positive, productive visions of the future without seeing the contexts of despair out of which they arise or into which they sink.

a systematic future works within a fiction can also be powerful.

What perspective to take on the world of the future? If the problems you are addressing are large-scale and systematic, a wide-angle or "god game" view may be best, as long as it can be done without leaving human concerns behind. If you want to appeal to personal and social benefits of your vision, focusing on an individual, or a day in a person's life, might be right. If you're trying to improve the type of life you have and the type of work you do—as a researcher or inventor, for instance—show how you yourself would like to work, and use your advances to bootstrap yourself.

Where to set one's imagination of the future? Moving one's future vision to a different sort of place, a utopia, can allow critical engagement with today's society and help to dislodge our thinking from well-worn ruts. But whether or not one's imagination moves off to nowhere, don't discard the social world, the everyday values and practices in which new technologies are embedded.

How do initially fine-grained ideas about the future grow? On a lattice of principles, high-level goals, and systematic thinking. Whether one's goal is a self-sufficient house or a system for augmenting human intellect, having the overarching goal in mind and developing systematic ways of thinking about that goal provide specific guidance on which directions to pursue and how to pursue them.

What allows ideas about the future to take root? It's a great benefit if they are free and open to use and share. It's harder for people to agree to invest their time and thought in a system that someone else owns and controls, which may be shuttered when a startup goes out of business or when someone with different ideas and values takes control.

Do models of the future need to be reasonable and lead to positive outcomes? Perhaps at some stage realistic models will come in handy, but visions of the future have proved to be useful even if they are rather absurd and exaggerated, and can highlight the negative consequences of current trends. It's possible that exaggeration is even necessary to make the point at times, or to help us enlarge our imagination.

I do encourage thinkers to use all sorts of media to imagine the future, and to share their imaginations of the future. And, I suppose it's as easy to say "the future is unbuilt" or "the future has not yet been designed" as it is to say "the future is unwritten." But I also suspect, as fascinating as design fiction videos, TV series, and world's fair exhibitions have been, that we will still have a lot of writing to do as we work together to develop a better future. Plenty of the imagining we do, the sharing of that imagination,

Perhaps at some stage realistic models will come in handy, but visions of the future have proved to be useful even if they are rather absurd and exaggerated, and can highlight the negative consequences of current trends. It's possible that exaggeration is even necessary to make the point at times, or to help us enlarge our imagination.

and the revision and reimagining we do together will surely be done by putting words together. I hope *The Future* serves as one useful, effective part of that work, offering lessons in future-making that will inform and encourage you as you read this conclusion and close this book— and turn to that next, important volume, the one that is unwritten.

NOTES

Preface

1. For another take on how the future has been viewed in the United States, see Samuel 2009, which traces through U.S. cultural attitudes to the future in the twentieth century. Samuel fits several of the technological topics of this book into a broader historical framework; his focus is on historicizing cultural attitudes in the United States, though, and is not the same as mine: uncovering principles and practices for future-making.

2. After I wrote this book and just before it went to press, Jennifer Gidley's short book, also entitled *The Future* (but with the subtitle "A Very Short Introduction"), was published (Gidley 2017). For those interested in academic and research approaches to the future of this sort, Gidley seems an ideal person to discuss them, as she is president of the World Futures Studies Federation.

1 Facing the Future

1. This translation is from Benjamin 1989. This essay is also known as "On the Concept of History."

2. Núñez and Sweetser 2006.

3. This phrase appeared on the record sleeve of the Clash's 1982 album, *Combat Rock*. It became strongly associated with Strummer and with the Clash's particular take on punk, which acknowledged grim realities but also rejected hopelessness, seeing the possibility for political improvement. The phrase was used to title an academic article (Bindas 1993) and as the subtitle to an award-winning documentary about Strummer (Temple 2007).

4. Holliday 2001.

5. Novak 2008.

6. For a nuanced look at how ideas of the future are wrapped up in our social and cultural past, see Augé 2015. In this book, he considers the relationship of the future and supposedly forward-thinking ideas to current anxieties and social structures. Among other things, he delivers an interesting critique of the supposedly liberating open-plan office which, in combination with long-standing hierarchies, actually leads workers to be "imprisoned by the gaze of other people" rather than freeing them to view the horizon (55).

7. Eveleth 2015.

2 Oracles, Prophecy, and Divination

1. Hasker 1989, 194.
2. Jaynes 1976, 240.
3. Heilbroner 1995, 31.
4. Ibid., 69.
5. The discussion in philosophy about whether people can make decisions, or whether everything is determined, is covered in another MIT Press Essential Knowledge book (Balaguer 2014).

3 Literary Utopias

1. This is the first of three major utopian fictions I discuss. The first one is listed in the bibliography in two editions as More [1516] 1965 and More 2012. The other two are Bellamy [1888] 2003 and Gilman [1915] 2014.
2. Goodman 2008, 15.
3. One compelling antecedent to Gilman's feminist utopia was written by Margaret Cavendish, duchess of Newcastle, and originally published in 1666. The book is prototypical of science fiction and is known as *The Blazing World* (Cavendish 1991).
4. A powerful argument has been made about how the power of spectacle and imagination, reaching well into the absurd, can be effectively used for progressive purposes. See Duncombe 2007.

4 Words-in-Freedom, Art for the Future

1. Perloff 1986, 89–90.
2. This manifesto and the founding manifesto of Futurism are among the many collected and provided in English translation in Caws 2001.
3. Gentile 2003, 41.
4. Berghaus 2009, 27.
5. Quoted in Poggi 2009, 148.

5 World's Fairs and Exhibiting the Future

1. Early national and international exhibitions, and documentation of them, are covered in Carpenter 1972.
2. The main single reference for all the official world's fairs, beginning with the 1851 Great Exhibition in London, is Findling and Pelle 2008.
3. Morshed 2001.

6 The Pre-invention of the Web

1. Nelson 1990; Nelson 1974.
2. Nelson 1999.

7 The Computer Becomes a Book

1. A very good, long retrospective study of the Dynabook project is provided in Maxwell 2006.
2. Campbell-Kelly and Aspray 1996.
3. Montfort 2016.
4. Kay 1972.
5. Kay and Goldberg 2003; originally published in 1977.
6. Ibid.
7. Kay 1972.
8. Kay 1993.
9. Ibid.
10. For a critical perspective on OLPC, see Kraemer, Dedrick, and Sharma 2009. For the first empirical results on the program's effects on access to computing, and on cognitive development, see the study done in Peru by Cristia et al. 2012.

8 Current Fictions

1. Eames 1972.
2. Bleecker 2009.
3. Eames 1972.
4. Corning 2011.

REFERENCES

Augé, Marc. 2015. *The Future*. Trans. John Howe. Brooklyn, NY, and London: Verso Books.

Balaguer, Mark. 2014. *Free Will*. Cambridge, MA, and London: MIT Press.

Bel Geddes, Norman. 1940. *Magic Motorways*. New York: Random House.

Bellamy, Edward. [1888] 2003. *Looking Backward: 2000–1887*. Ed. Alex MacDonald. Peterborough, ON: Broadview Press.

Benjamin, Walter. 1989. "Theses on the Philosophy of History." In *Critical Theory and Society: A Reader*, ed. S. E. Bronner and D. M. Kellner, 255–263. New York: Routledge, 1989.

Berghaus, Gunter. 2009. "Futurism and the Technological Imagination: Poised between Machine Cult and Machine Angst." In *Futurism and the Technological Imagination*, ed. Gunter Berghaus, 1–39. Amsterdam and New York: Éditions Rodopi.

Bindas, Kenneth J. 1993. "'The Future is Unwritten': *The Clash*, Punk, and America, 1977–1982." *American Studies* 34 (1): 69–89.

Bleecker, Julian. 2009. "Design Fiction: A Short Essay on Design, Science, Fact and Fiction." Near Future Laboratory. http://blog.nearfuturelaboratory.com/2009/03/17/design-fiction-a-short-essay-on-design-science-fact-and-fiction/.

Brooker, Charlie. 2014–. *Black Mirror*. TV Series. Channel 4, 2011–2013. Netflix.

Campbell-Kelly, Martin, and William Aspray. 1996. *Computer: A History of the Information Machine*. New York: Basic Books/HarperCollins.

Carpenter, Kenneth E. 1972. "European Industrial Exhibitions before 1851 and Their Publications." *Technology and Culture* 13 (3): 465–486. doi:10.2307/3102498.

Cavendish, Margaret. 1991. *The Description of the New Blazing World and Other Writings*. London: Pickering & Chatto.

Caws, Mary Ann, ed. 2001. *Manifesto: A Century of Isms*. Lincoln: University of Nebraska Press.

Corning. 2011. *A Day Made of Glass*. Video, 5:32. https://www.youtube.com/watch?v=6Cf7IL_eZ38.

Cristia, Julian, Pablo Ibarrarán, Santiago Cueto, Ana Santiago, and Eugenio Severín. 2012. "Technology and Child Development: Evidence from the One Laptop Per Child Program." IDB Working Paper No. IDB-WP-304. April 1. https://papers.ssrn.com/sol3/papers.cfm?abstract_id=2032444.

Duncombe, Stephen. 2007. *Dream: Re-imagining Progressive Politics in an Age of Fantasy*. New York: The New Press.

Dunne, Anthony, and Fiona Raby. 2013. *Speculative Everything: Design, Fiction, and Social Dreaming*. Cambridge, MA, and London: MIT Press.

Eames, Charles. 1972. *Design Q & A*. Color film, 5:00. The Eames Office. https://www.youtube.com/watch?v=3xYi2rd1QCg.

Eveleth, Rose. 2015. "Why the 'Kitchen of the Future' Always Fails Us." *Eater*. September 15. http://www.eater.com/2015/9/15/9326775/the-kitchen-of-the-future-has-failed-us.

Findling, John E., and Kimberly D. Pelle, eds. 2008. *Encyclopedia of World's Fairs and Expositions*. Jefferson, NC, and London: McFarland.

Gentile, Emilio. 2003. *The Struggle for Modernity: Nationalism, Futurism, and Fascism*. Santa Barbara, CA: Greenwood Publishing Group.

Gidley, Jennifer. 2017. *The Future: A Very Short Introduction*. Oxford: Oxford University Press.

Gilman, Charlotte Perkins. [1915] 2014. *Herland and Selected Stories*. New York: Penguin.

Goodman, Donna. 2008. *A History of the Future*. New York: Monacelli Press.

Hasker, William. 1989. *God, Time, and Knowledge*. Ithaca: Cornell University Press.

Heilbroner, Robert. 1995. *Visions of the Future: The Distant Past, Yesterday, Today, Tomorrow*. New York: Oxford University Press.

Holliday, Laura Scott. 2001. "Kitchen Technologies: Promises and Alibis, 1944–1966." *Camera Obscura* 16 (2): 1–131.

Jaynes, Julian. 1976. *The Origin of Consciousness in the Breakdown of the Bicameral Mind*. Boston: Houghton Mifflin.

Kay, Alan C. 1972. "A Personal Computer for Children of All Ages." In *Proceedings of the ACM Annual Conference*, vol. 1. New York: ACM. http://delivery.acm.org/10.1145/1980000/1971922/a1-kay72.pdf?ip=18.76.1.17&id=1971922&acc=ACTIVE%20SERVICE&key=7777116298C9657D%2EDE5F786C30E1A3B4%2E4D4702B0C3E38B35%2E4D4702B0C3E38B35&CFID=785220182&CFTOKEN=41897080&__acm__=1499958234_1e5f2cc4b38d7509a0178ccd3aa464e1.

Kay, Alan C. 1993. "The Early History of Smalltalk." History of Programming Languages II, Cambridge, MA, April 20–23. http://gagne.homedns.org/~tgagne/contrib/EarlyHistoryST.html.

Kay, Alan, and Adele Goldberg. 2003. "Personal Dynamic Media." In *The New Media Reader*, ed. Noah Wardrip-Fruin and Nick Montfort, 391–404. Cambridge, MA, and London: MIT Press. http://www.newmediareader.com/book_samples/nmr-26-kay.pdf.

Kraemer, Kenneth L., Jason Dedrick, and Prakul Sharma. 2009. "One Laptop Per Child: Vision vs. Reality." *Communications of the ACM* 52 (6): 66–73. http://globalize.pbworks.com/f/OneLaptopVisionvsReality.pdf.

Marinetti, F. T. 1909. "The Futurist Manifesto." Trans. James Joll. http://bactra.org/T4PM/futurist-manifesto.html.

Maxwell, John W. 2006. "Tracing the Dynabook: A Study of Technocultural Transformations." PhD diss., University of British Columbia. https://open.library.ubc.ca/cIRcle/collections/ubctheses/831/items/1.0055157.

Metz, Cade. 2008. "The Mother of All Demos—150 Years Ahead of Its Time." *The Register*, December 11. http://www.theregister.co.uk/2008/12/11/engelbart_celebration/.

Montfort, Nick. 2016. "Batch/Interactive." In *Time: A Vocabulary of the Present*, ed. Joel Burges and Amy J. Elias. New York: New York University Press.

More, Thomas. [1516] 1965. *Utopia*. Trans. P. Turner. Baltimore: Penguin.

More, Thomas. 2012. *The Open Utopia*. Ed. Stephen Duncombe. http://theopenutopia.org.

Morshed, Adnan Zillur. 2001. "The Aviator's (Re)vision of the World: An Aesthetics of Ascension in Norman Bel Geddes's Futurama." PhD diss., Massachusetts Institute of Technology.

Nelson, Theodor H. 1974. *Computer Lib/Dream Machines*. Published by the author.

Nelson, Theodor H. 1990. *Literary Machines 90.1*. Published by the author.

Nelson, Ted. 1999. "Ted Nelson's Computer Paradigm, Expressed as One-Liners." http://xanadu.com.au/ted/TN/WRITINGS/TCOMPARADIGM/tedCompOneLiners.html.

Novak, Matt. 2008. "Tomorrow's Kitchen (1943)." *Paleo-Future*. http://paleo-future.blogspot.com/2008/12/tomorrows-kitchen-1943.html.

Núñez, Rafael E., and Eve Sweetser. 2006. "With the Future behind Them: Convergent Evidence from Aymara Language and Gesture in the Crosslinguistic Comparison of Spatial Construals of Time." *Cognitive Science* 30 (3): 401–450.

Perloff, Marjorie. 1986. *The Futurist Moment: Avant-Garde, Avant Guerre, and the Language of Rupture, with a New Preface*. Chicago: University of Chicago Press.

Poggi, Christine. 2009. *Inventing Futurism: The Art and Politics of Artificial Optimism*. Princeton University Press.

Rainey, L., C. Poggi, and L. Wittman, eds. 2009. *Futurism: An Anthology*. New Haven: Yale University Press.

Samuel, Lawrence R. 2009. *Future: A Recent History*. Austin: University of Texas Press.

Sterling, Bruce. 2005. *Shaping Things*. Mediaworks Pamphlet series. Cambridge, MA, and London: MIT Press.

Temple, Julian, dir. 2007. *Joe Strummer: The Future Is Unwritten*. Documentary feature film. Eagle Farm, Queensland: Magna Pacific.

Wardrip-Fruin, N., and N. Montfort, eds. 2003. *The New Media Reader*. Cambridge, MA, and London: MIT Press.

INDEX

NICK MONTFORT develops computational art and poetry. His computer-generated books of poetry include *#!*, the collaboration *2×6*, *Autopia*, and (forthcoming) *The Truelist*. Among his more than fifty digital projects are the collaborations *The Deletionist*, *Sea and Spar Between*, and *Renderings*. His MIT Press books, collaborative and individual, are *The New Media Reader*, *Twisty Little Passages*, *Racing the Beam*, *10 PRINT CHR$(205.5+RND(1));: GOTO 10*, and most recently *Exploratory Programming for the Arts and Humanities*. He is professor of digital media at MIT and lives in New York and Boston.